Poetry and Pearls II

Romantic Poetry

by

N.R.Hart

Monday Creek Publishing LLC
mondaycreekpublishing.com

Cover Illustration by Logan Rogers

N.R.Hart logo design by R.A. Cantu

ISBN: 9780578428666

DEDICATION

"If I love you then I
will turn you into poetry..."
-N.R.Hart

"Souls tend to go back to who
feels like home."
-N.R.Hart

Table of Contents

INTRODUCTION

We have only one heart yet the heart holds all four seasons inside. Winter can be a time of solitude. Spring a time of carefree fancy. Summer a time of fun and youthfulness and Autumn our souls take flight.

Our hearts can survive the harshest of winters only to breathe in the sweetest scents of spring. There is a stillness inside all of us. Whether we choose to stop and listen to it, not everyone knows how. Poetry is used to express this stillness inside of us and fill the spaces between us with the words we are unable to say. Poetry can take us to a vulnerable place inside, allowing us to experience our innermost turbulence in the gentlest of ways. Our hearts speak to us every day, listen carefully to what it has to say. Come with me on this journey of the heart. The seasons of my heart and yours.

"Pay attention to what speaks to your heart."

N.R.Hart

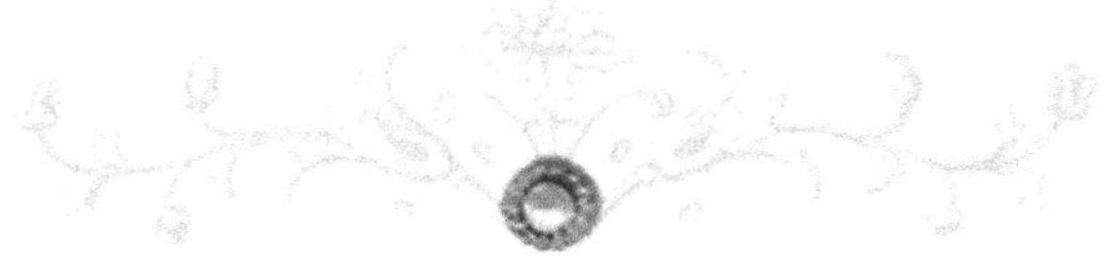

A Winter Season

"You are written on my heart

in permanent ink."

N.R.Hart

You are all that is unearthly and dazzling
like burning stars or symphonies in rain
a walk in springtime, a sweet summer
romance
crisp autumn leaves that never stop falling
you are the soft wind, a silent winter waltz
shivering in a crimson kiss, like fire and ice.
You are poetry in bloom. You are the seasons
of my heart. You exist in me everywhere.

-N.R.Hart "seasons of the heart"

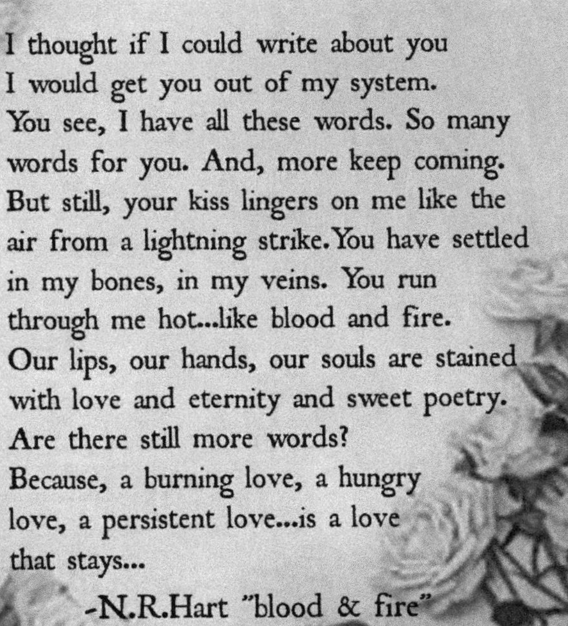
I thought if I could write about you
I would get you out of my system.
You see, I have all these words. So many
words for you. And, more keep coming.
But still, your kiss lingers on me like the
air from a lightning strike. You have settled
in my bones, in my veins. You run
through me hot...like blood and fire.
Our lips, our hands, our souls are stained
with love and eternity and sweet poetry.
Are there still more words?
Because, a burning love, a hungry
love, a persistent love...is a love
that stays...
-N.R.Hart "blood & fire"

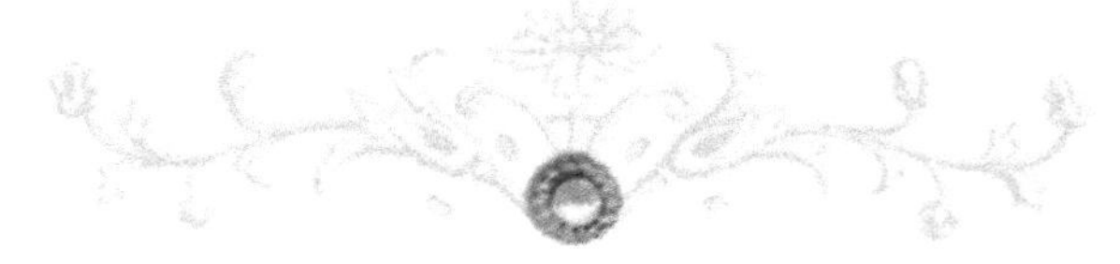

Beauty and the Beast by N.R.Hart

Legend has it
there is always a reason why souls meet.
Maybe, they found each other
for reasons that weren't so different
after all.
They were two souls searching
and found a home lost in each other.
When souls find comfort in one another
separation is not possible.
The reasons they are brought together
are no accident...
Maybe she needed someone
to show her how to live
and he needed someone
to show him how to love. -N.R.Hart ©

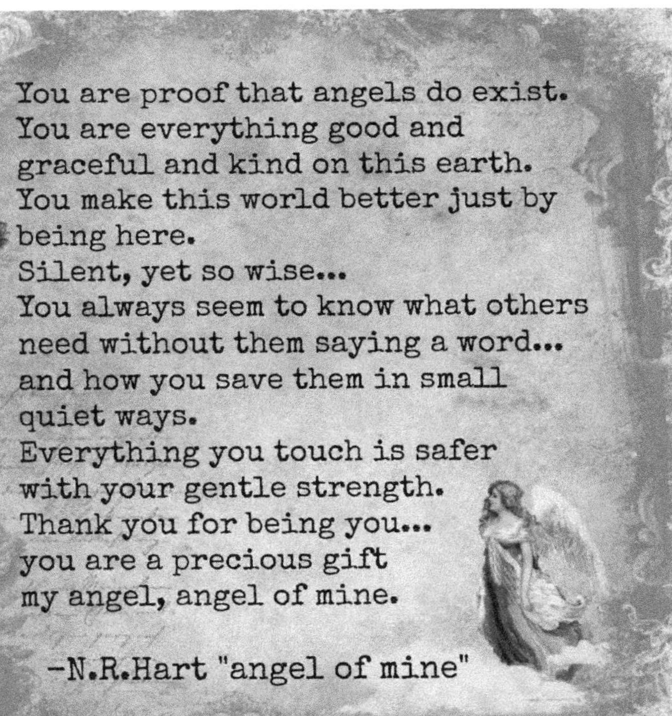
You are proof that angels do exist.
You are everything good and
graceful and kind on this earth.
You make this world better just by
being here.
Silent, yet so wise...
You always seem to know what others
need without them saying a word...
and how you save them in small
quiet ways.
Everything you touch is safer
with your gentle strength.
Thank you for being you...
you are a precious gift
my angel, angel of mine.

-N.R.Hart "angel of mine"

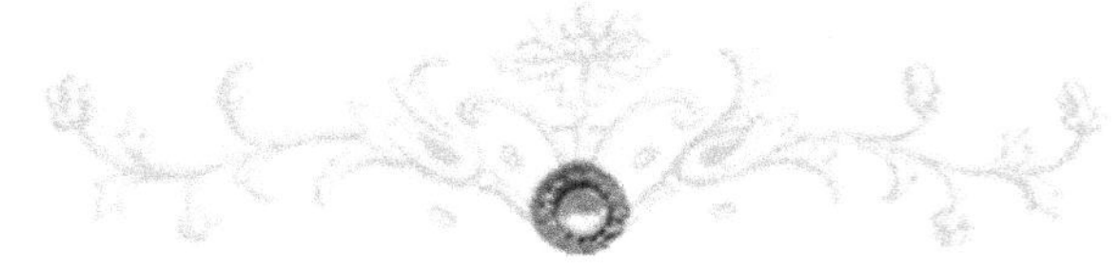

"Healer"

All she had were her words
to give them...
she found them buried deep
in her bones
she bared everything for them
so she could ease their pain...
make them feel less alone.
She wanted to comfort them
heal their souls...
so they wouldn't carry that pain
home.

-N.R.Hart

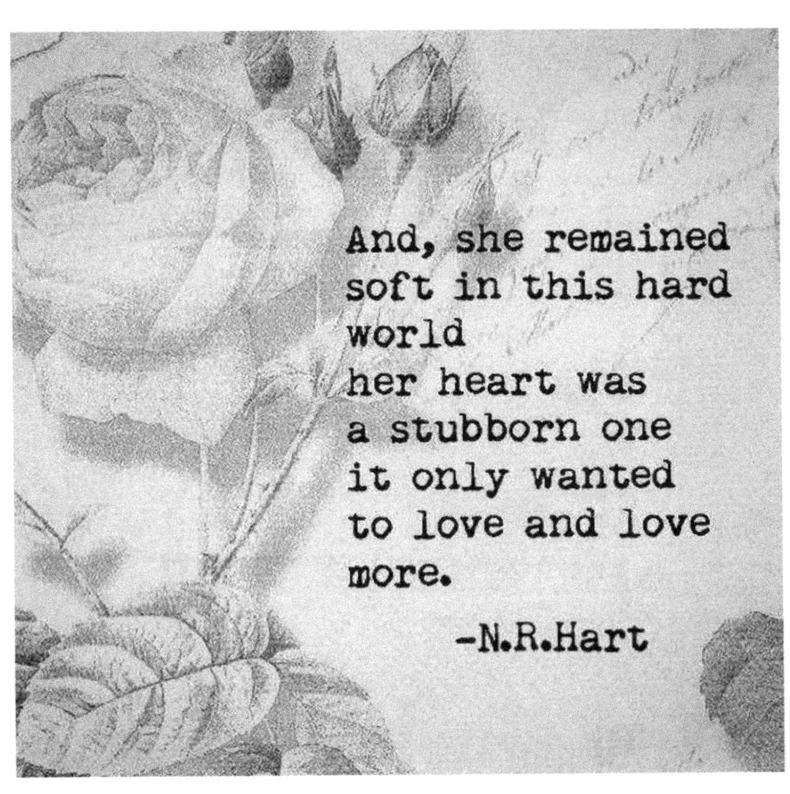
And, she remained
soft in this hard
world
her heart was
a stubborn one
it only wanted
to love and love
more.
-N.R.Hart

A love letter - part2

This is a love letter to those I have loved before.
And, I am certain of only one thing. It was I, who
loved you, with everything I had. I was vulnerable
with you. I lost control over you. I handed over
my heart, offered my soul for the taking.
I wrote poems about you. Can you say the same?
And, it is a scary notion to think just how much
love was lost, because you feared loving me back
with the same fierceness that I loved you.
I had nothing to do with it, my soul chose you,
therefore, I loved you too. It was our time
together. And, we had the rarest kind of love...
a soul love.
And, sometimes you don't realize that time , that
unfathomable moment, while you are living it...
and then it is gone forever. And, now...now
you can look back on all those precious moments
that were lost because you were too afraid to
love me...
Read my poems and ache for me. And, in the years
to come...when the light is gone from your eyes...
you will remember me...and our fire. -N.R.Hart

If a writer loves you,
they will write about things others never notice.
They will write about how the light prisms in your
eyes bounce off the sun changing color each time
you smile.
They will write about how the very nearness of you
causes a rapid change in their breathing pattern.
They will gaze into your eyes deeper until
you feel their soul penetrating your soul.
Their touch lingers on you the longest as the heat
brands a memory on each layer of your skin.
They will write about what resembles you so closely
you will find out things you never knew about
yourself.
If a writer loves you...they will love you
so fiercely you will not likely ever feel passion
like this again in your lifetime. They will describe
every mesmerizing detail about the ecstasy
of loving you, as they swallow all your words
savoring the taste of them, so they cannot forget.
And, neither can you. -N.R.Hart

"if a writer loves you"

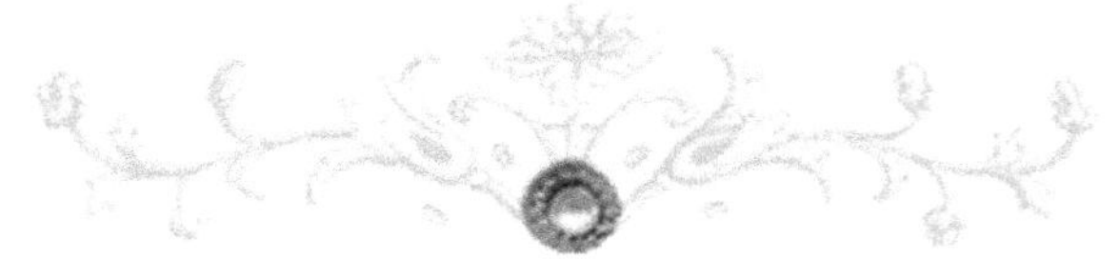

You appeared in my life out
of nowhere.
I never saw you coming yet
I have felt you here
my whole life.
All this time I thought
I was the one saving you but
like guardian angels who work
in mysterious ways...
I now know we were saving
each other instead.

-N.R.Hart "guardian angel"

Some things take time...
move softly, move gracefully.
Be gentle with yourself.
Listen to your soul...
for it knows how to heal
you. -N.R.Hart

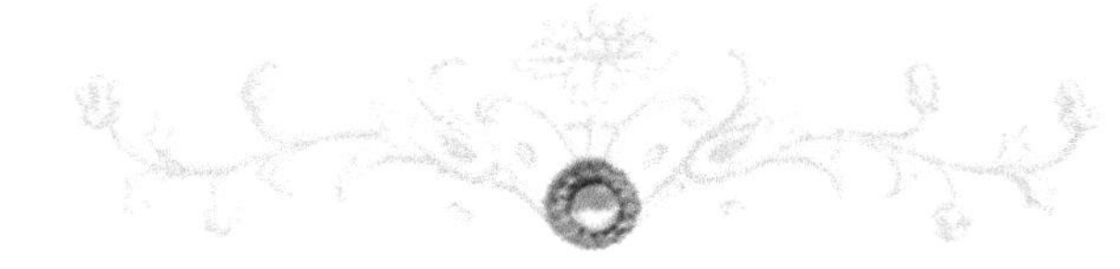

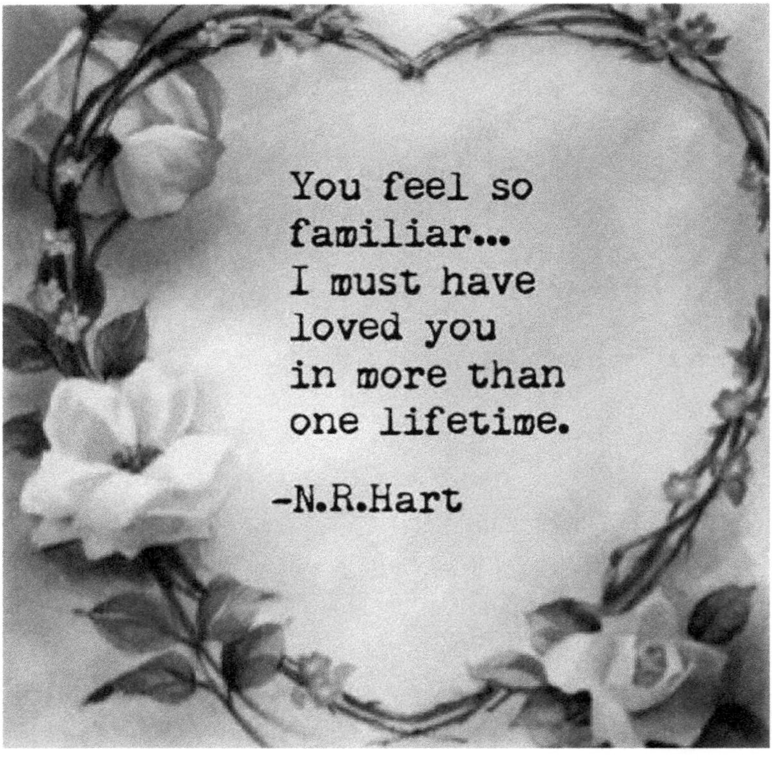

You feel so
familiar...
I must have
loved you
in more than
one lifetime.

-N.R.Hart

She is always in love with
the broken souls...
the ones who feel too much
carry too much pain inside
their hearts breaking every day
for something or someone...
and oftentimes she thought
she was the one trying to fix them
but now she has come to realize
that it was her own reflection
she saw in their eyes.

N.R.Hart / "reflection"

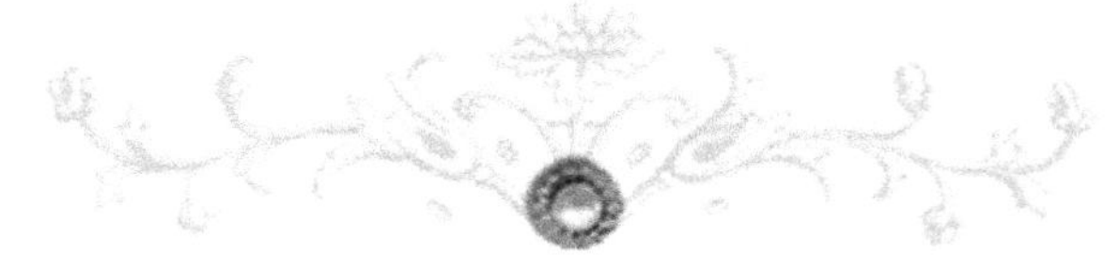

She knew deep down
she couldn't save
the world
but how beautiful
was it that she never
stopped trying.

-N.R.Hart

•

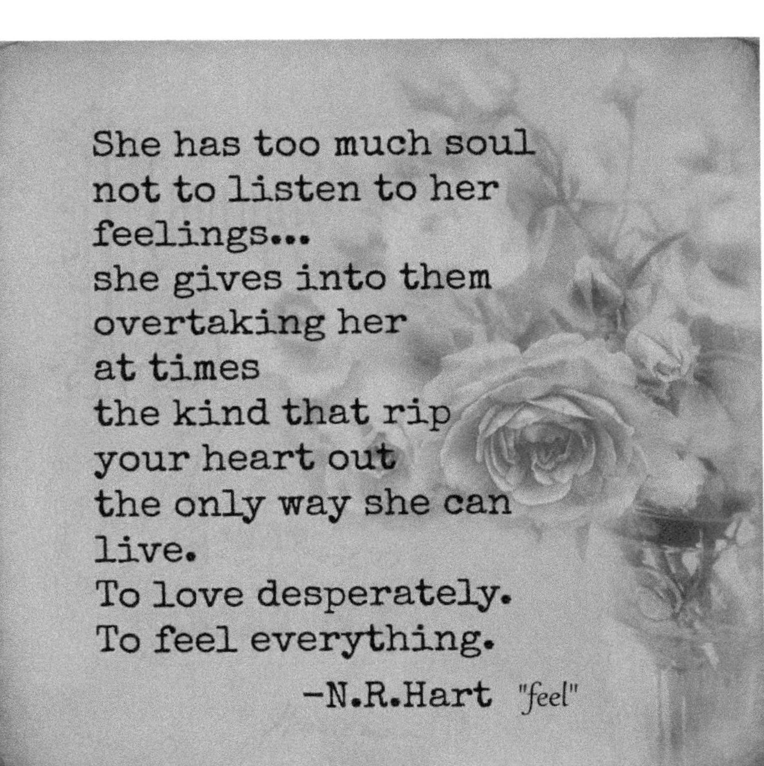
She has too much soul
not to listen to her
feelings...
she gives into them
overtaking her
at times
the kind that rip
your heart out
the only way she can
live.
To love desperately.
To feel everything.
-N.R.Hart "feel"

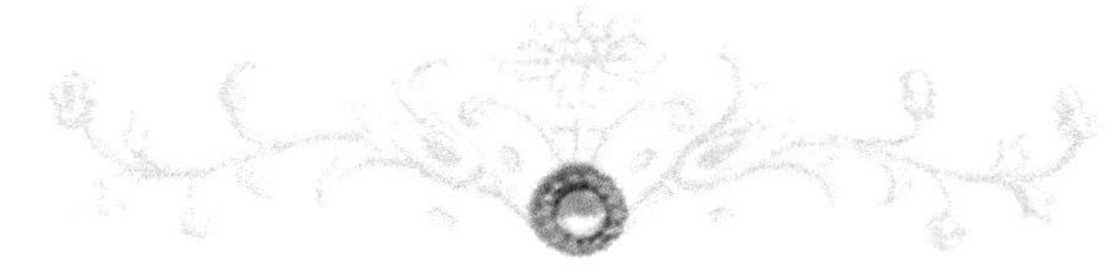

Try as she might she could not
get him out of her head
he was still there rummaging
through her thoughts
rearranging her messy heart
his breath planting wild violets
underneath her thirsty skin
laying claim to her yearnful soul
she wonders if he has any idea
of his affect on her, and if so
why...how...is he not here?

-N.R. Hart

"wild violets"

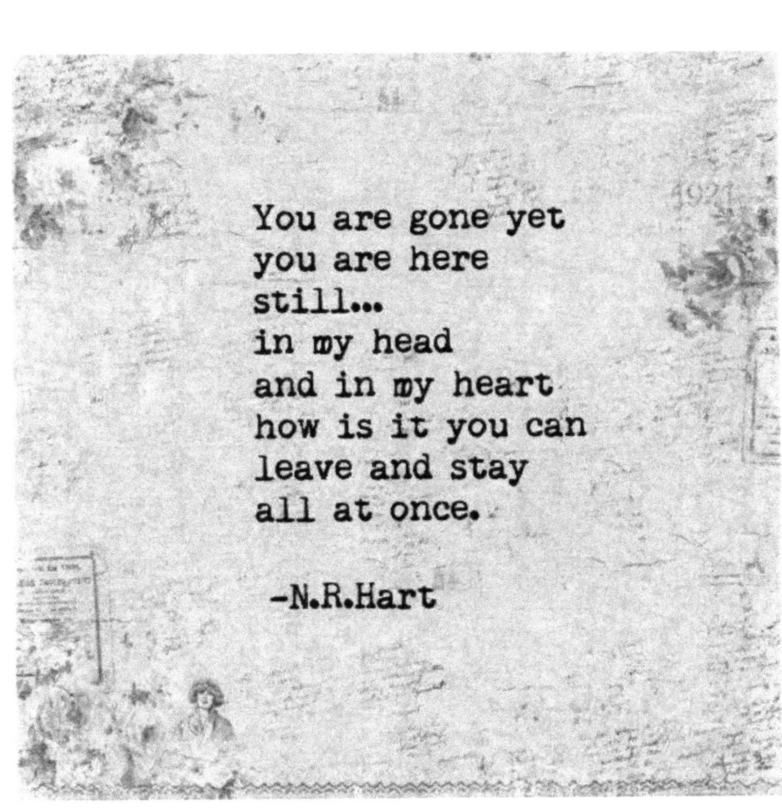
You are gone yet
you are here
still...
in my head
and in my heart
how is it you can
leave and stay
all at once.

-N.R.Hart

Do you think you have
a choice in loving someone?
The answer will always be...no.
Your soul picks who you love
and your heart seals the deal.
How little a choice we have
over such things when
your heart knows what it wants
and your soul knows when it's real.
N.R. Hart
"heart and soul"

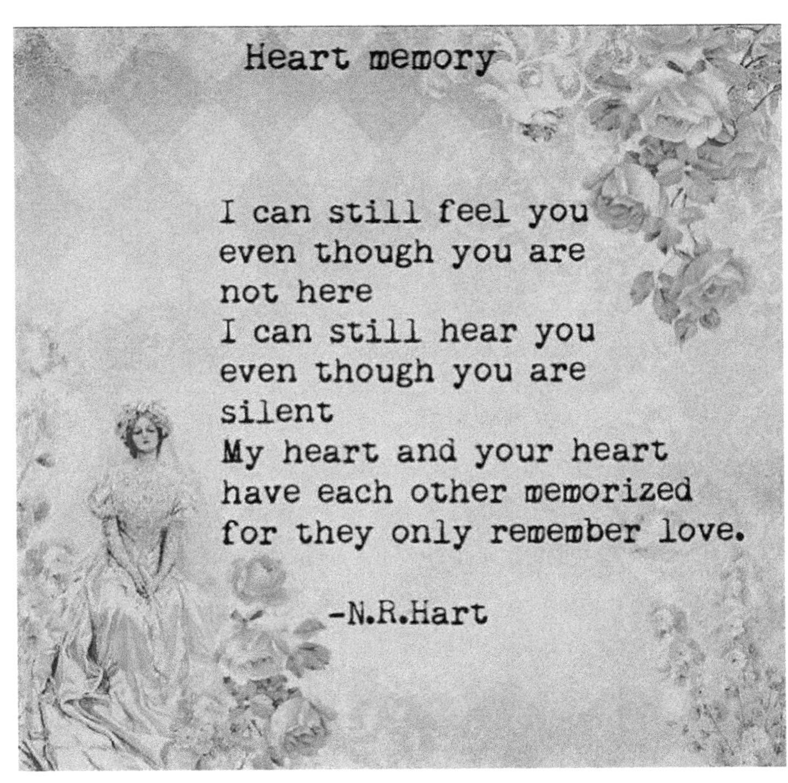
Heart memory
I can still feel you
even though you are
not here
I can still hear you
even though you are
silent
My heart and your heart
have each other memorized
for they only remember love.
-N.R.Hart

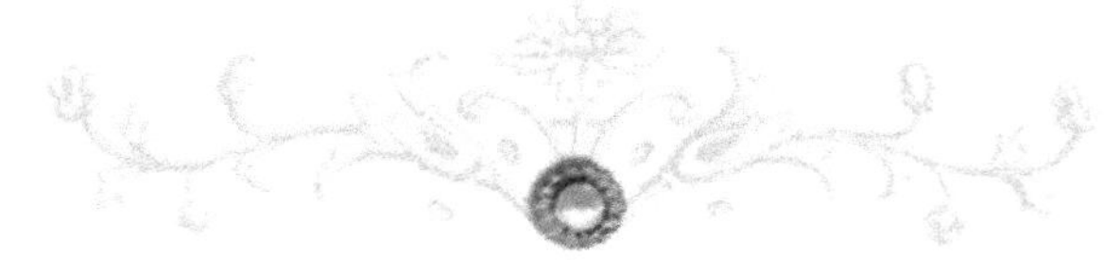

"spilled ink"

But darling,
they don't love
like you do...
And, therein lies your
problem.
Maybe your kind of love
doesn't exist anywhere but
in your mind and the ink
on this paper.

-N.R.Hart

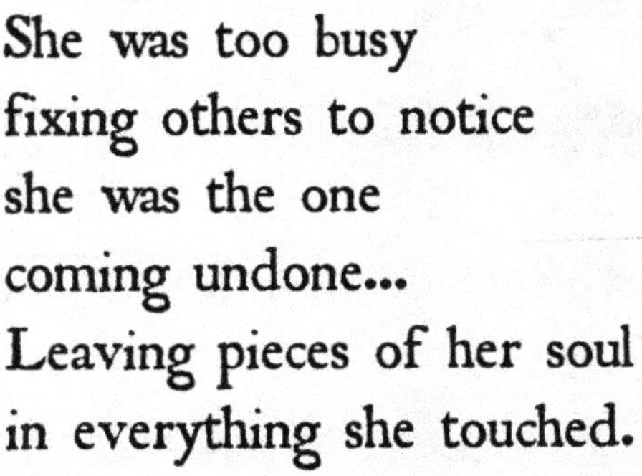
She was too busy
fixing others to notice
she was the one
coming undone...
Leaving pieces of her soul
in everything she touched.
N.R.Hart / "pieces of her soul"

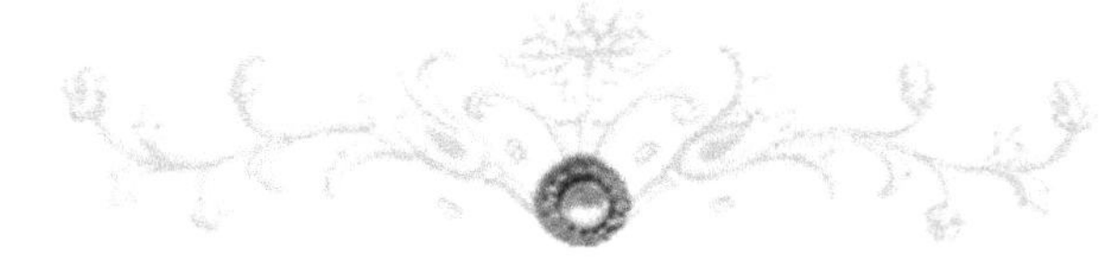

Loving someone deeply
fiercely, desperately
and now they are gone...
where does all that love go?

A love like that needs a home.

-N.R.Hart *"home"*

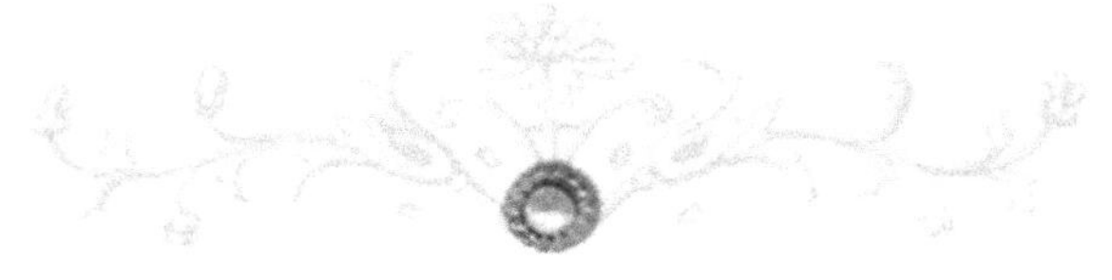

You always felt so familiar
as if we had known
one another
in every lifetime.
Except for this lifetime.
In this lifetime
you are a stranger that still
feels like home.

-N.R.Hart "familiar"

You broke me open
making me feel
things
lovely dark things
sweet heavenly things
and it has been
a long time
since I have felt
anything at all.

-N.R.Hart

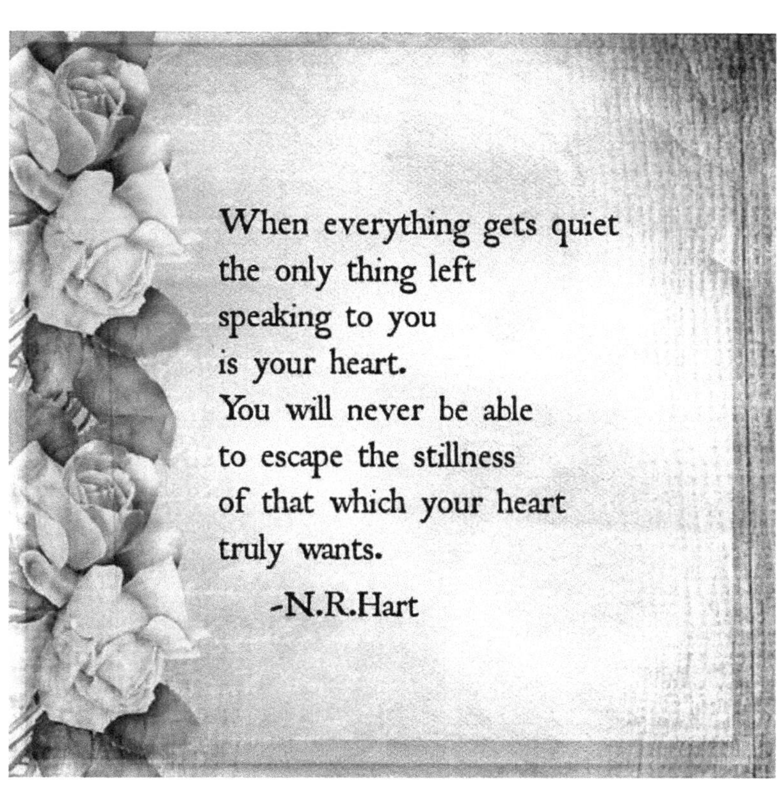
When everything gets quiet
the only thing left
speaking to you
is your heart.
You will never be able
to escape the stillness
of that which your heart
truly wants.
-N.R.Hart

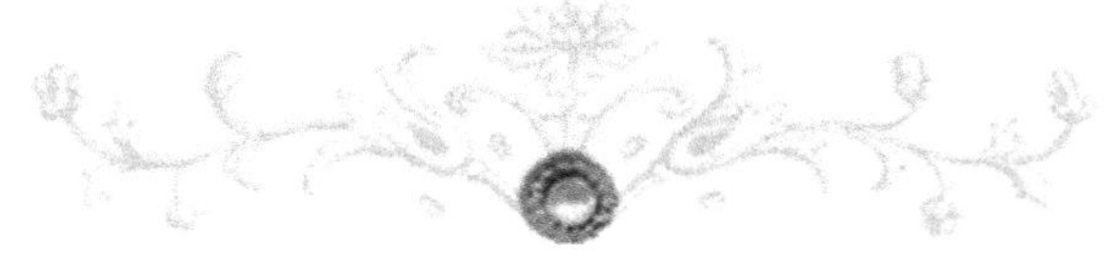

Somewhere in between
the silence and the
pain of missing you
broken hearts
keep beating love
against all will
and I believe
you loved me...and
I do love you still.

– N.R. Hart

"Having coffee"

They were just having coffee
except it wasn't really coffee
at all.
He was staring at her and she
was staring back at him
and it was hearts fluttering
and eyes flirting and cheeks
blushing.
It was more like souls
catching fire.
So in-between each sip of hot
steaming coffee
never mistake it for 'just coffee'
when they were secretly burning
for each other. -N.R.Hart

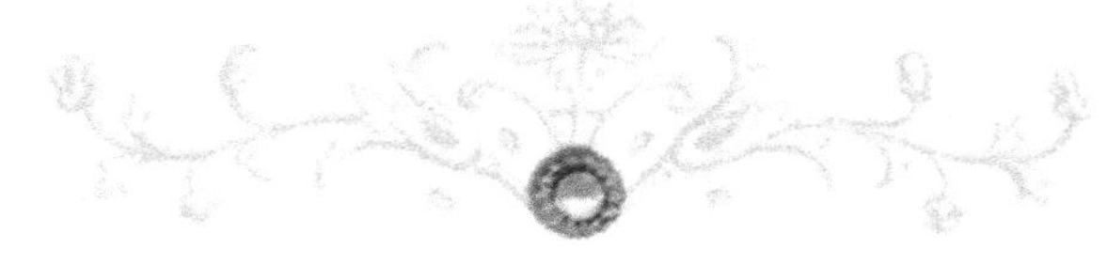

Distance

Creating all that distance
and your guarded way
of loving her
to protect your own heart
and you fell in love
with her anyway...

N.R.Hart

Beautiful Destruction

You destroyed me, every part of me,
split my soul in two and inside you
made me feel the most I had ever felt
before. I am not the same person for having
loved you...
You changed how I breathe, how I live,
how I love.
I am alive now and I feel everything.
I am the soft rains and the hard winds
the sweet mist and the heavy downpour
the burning sun and the chilled moon.
I exist in both darkness and light,
exhaling stars and fire.
And, I am burning in love. I fall to pieces.
I come undone. And, it was the most
beautiful destruction of all. -N.R.Hart

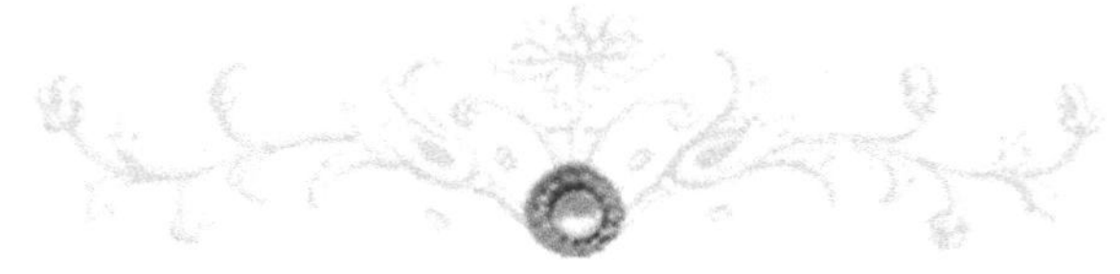

He always appears to her
in the warm moonlight
and the stillness shakes
with his presence
he is coming for her...
time slips away suddenly
and he is gone again
she is left wondering was it
real or just a dream...
still drenched in his warmth
she whispers into the darkness
what if he never knew how
precious he was to her.

-N.R.Hart / "dream"

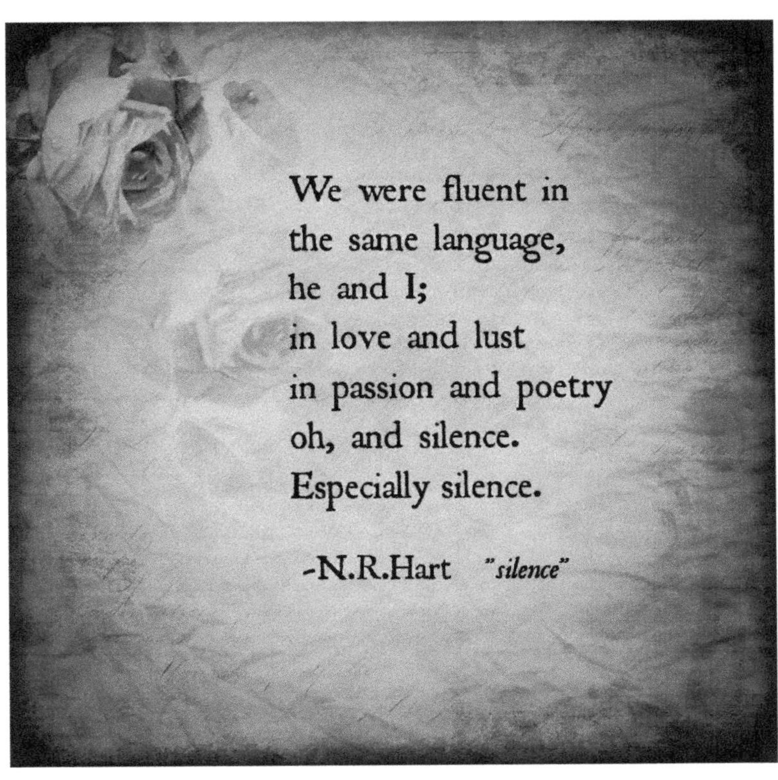
We were fluent in
the same language,
he and I;
in love and lust
in passion and poetry
oh, and silence.
Especially silence.
-N.R.Hart "silence"

You held me for the longest time
your arms persistent around me
a tight grip
and slowly it felt like all my pieces
with their sharp edges and jagged
breaths
began to soften and quiet
my soul hushed...
as the rest of the world disappeared
and for the first time in a long while...
This chaos was *home.*

-N.R.Hart "chaos"

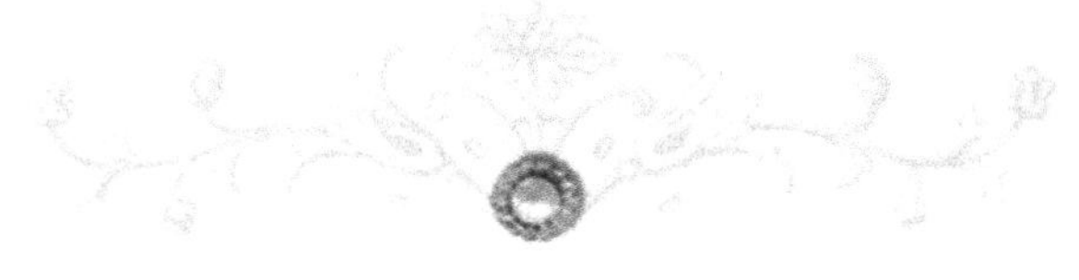

"She didn't know which way
to go as she clung to her
hopes and dreams so she held
on tight and let the wind carry
her soul instead. - N.R.Hart

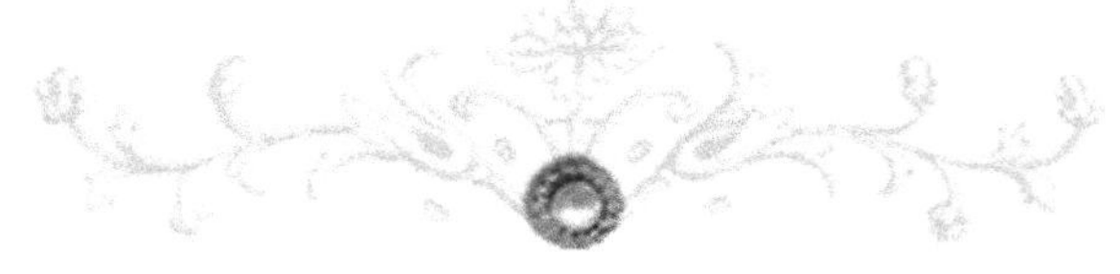

Sea of Love

She was just a girl
a poet a dreamer
a hopeless romantic
and never had she felt
so lost like a lone
pearl drowning in her
own sea of love.

- N.R.Hart

She is always too much...
she thinks too much, feels too much
she loves too much. Always too much...
of everything.
Yet, that did not stop her you see,
she needed for them to hear
her words of love...
She needed for them to feel something
again. Something they lost along
the way.
Maybe she couldn't save them, but
if she could make their world
a little softer, a little lighter,
then she would carry this burden
for the rest of them.
Because...she was in love with love
and she never understood how
the rest of the world wasn't in love...
the way she was. -N.R.Hart

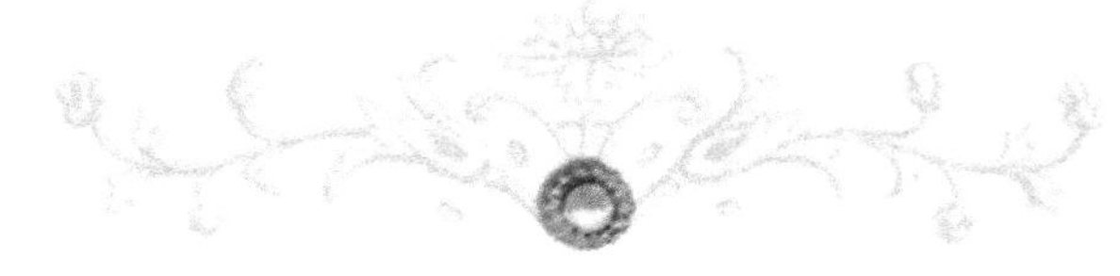

And if you cannot
find your way
out of the darkness
I will sit there
with you and
show you the stars.

-N.R.Hart

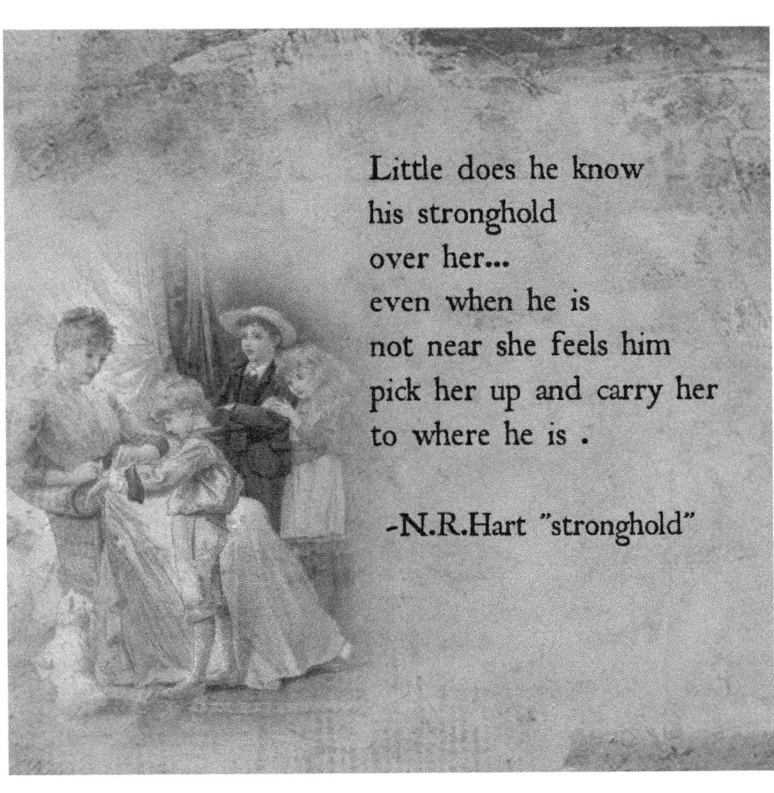
Little does he know
his stronghold
over her...
even when he is
not near she feels him
pick her up and carry her
to where he is .
-N.R.Hart "stronghold"

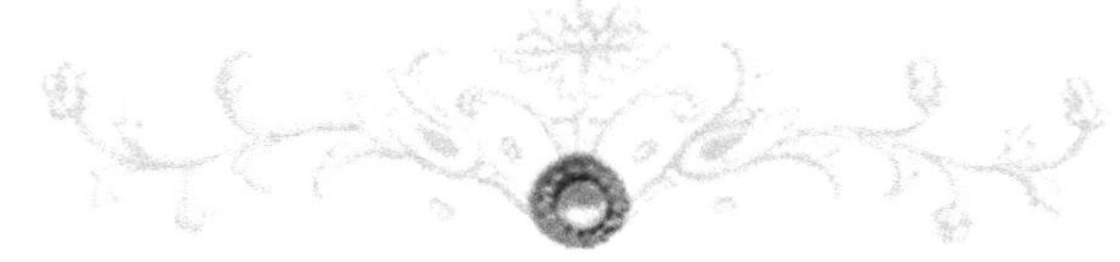

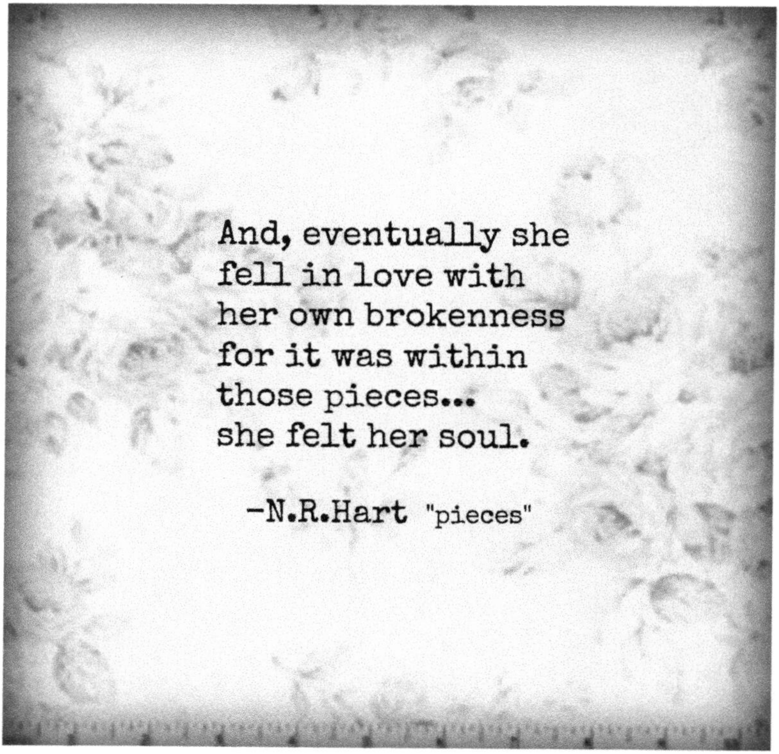

And, eventually she
fell in love with
her own brokenness
for it was within
those pieces...
she felt her soul.

-N.R.Hart "pieces"

All these things you love
you will never stop loving
you pour yourself into them
like the deep dark ocean
until they drown you
but, this is how you love
my dear,
and if it all comes crashing
down around you
you smile at the brilliant
shimmering pieces
because you loved them still
even when broken. *Even then.*

-N.R.Hart "shimmer"

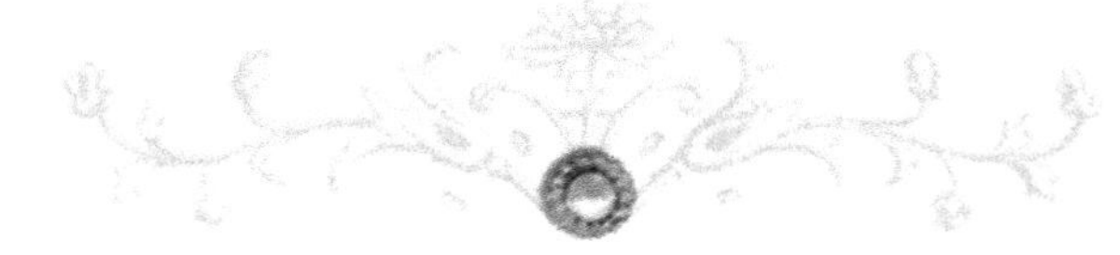

Once the soul loves
something or
someone
that kind of love
becomes irreplaceable.
-N.R.Hart

I think we always
gravitate back
to certain people
in our lives
because we feel
understood in their
presence and also
their silence.
-N.R.Hart
THE
Young Clerk
Assistant;
OR
PENMAN

COULDN'T YOU TELL
SHE ALWAYS
LOVED YOU
A LITTLE MORE
THAN
EVERYONE ELSE.
-N.R.HART

17, Rue de la République
Marseille
I have lived
a thousand lives
loving you...
and I have died
a thousand deaths
trying to forget you.
-N.R.Hart

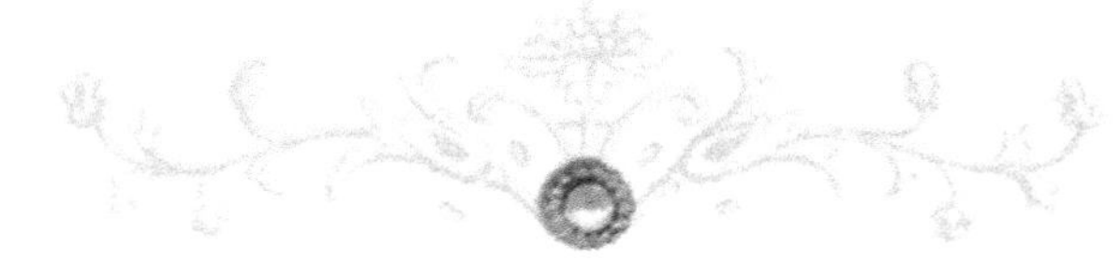

Winter Blues

And tonight,
tonight I need
a break from
all this fire
and when tomorrow
comes I will be
fierce once more
and slay some
dragons.

-N.R.Hart

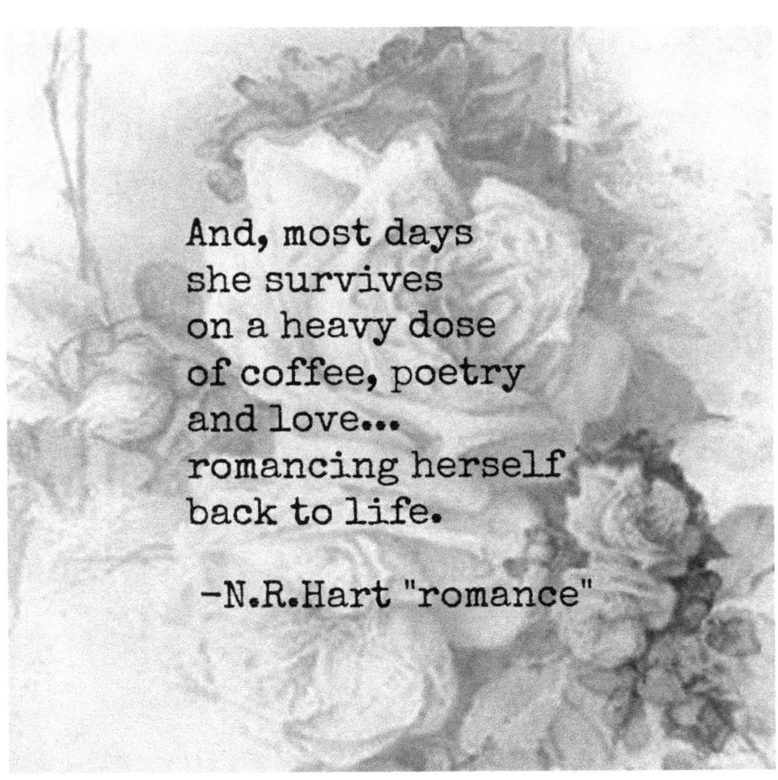
And, most days
she survives
on a heavy dose
of coffee, poetry
and love...
romancing herself
back to life.
-N.R.Hart "romance"

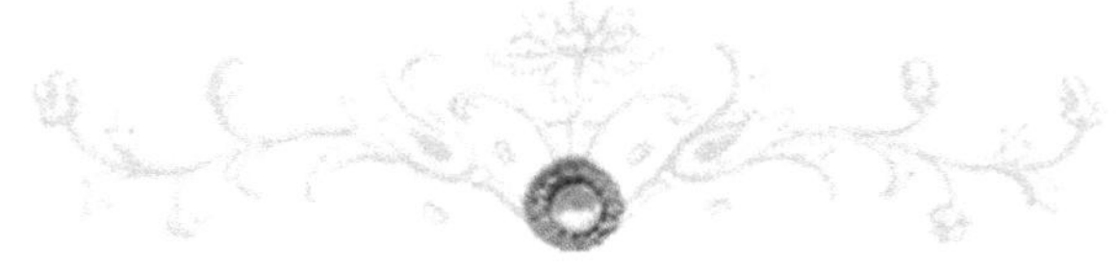

"Moonless Night"

How was I to know once you left
I would stop breathing.
You don't realize how necessary
breathing is until your air
has been taken from you.
Surely, you must be choking
on the smoke too?
The clouds have fallen
the sky is empty
I stare into a moonless night
and hold my breath
just waiting to inhale
yours again.

—N.R.Hart

"Legend"
As a girl she was
told to be seen
and not heard
then one day
she decided she had
much to say...
And became a legend
instead.
-N.R.Hart
PENMANSHI
POCKET-COPY-BOO
PARIS
10

Twin Flame
No matter where I go
my eyes will never stop
searching for you...
I am looking for the
other half of my soul.
-N.R.Hart

He said to her
don't fall in love
with me...
she thought
to herself
silly boy, we are best
friends...
we've been madly in love
since the day we met.
-N.R.Hart "Poetry and Pearls"

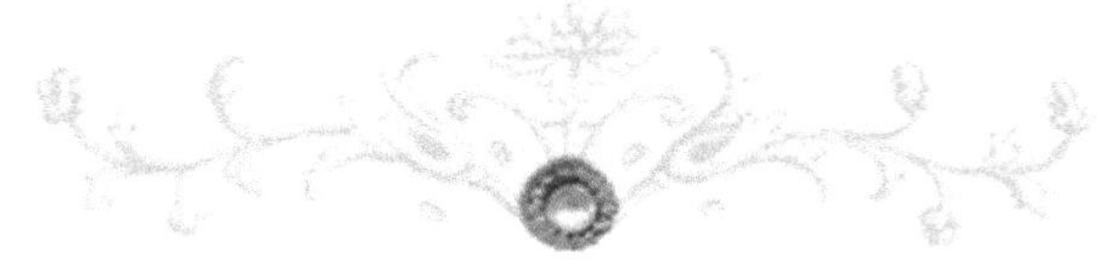

And i told him
i loved him
that i wrote him
into my story...
everything
i could not say...
it was our love story
yet he just turned
and walked away.
-N.R.Hart

Pay attention
to the message
the universe keeps
trying to send you...
for it was written
in the stars.
-N.R.Hart
"written in the stars"

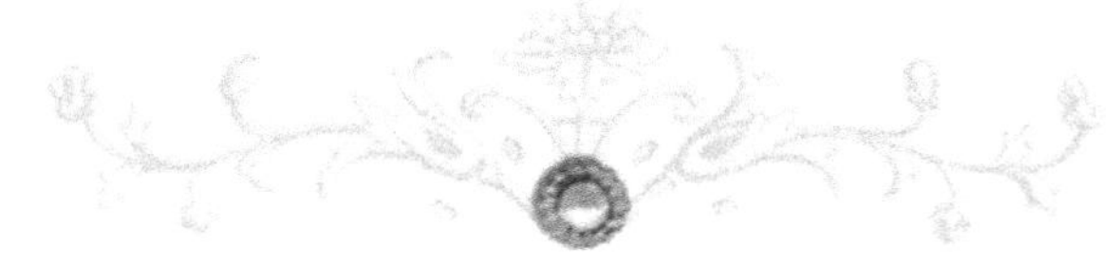

Muse

I write to keep this love alive.

-N.R.Hart

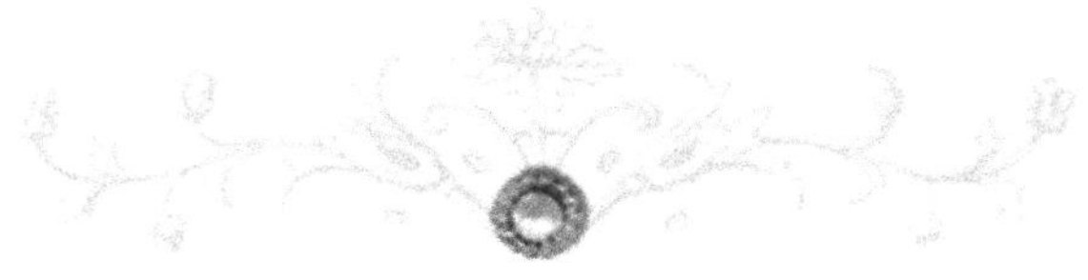

A Spring Season

"If I love you then, I will

turn you into poetry."

N.R.Hart

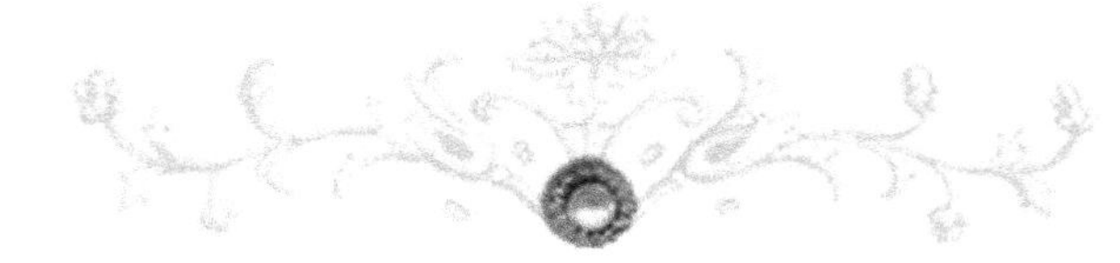

Kiss me
in the spring
so I know
what it feels like
to come alive
like a season.

-N.R.Hart / "alive"

She is always
too much...
she thinks too much
feels too much
she loves too much
always too much...
of everything.
- N.R. Hart

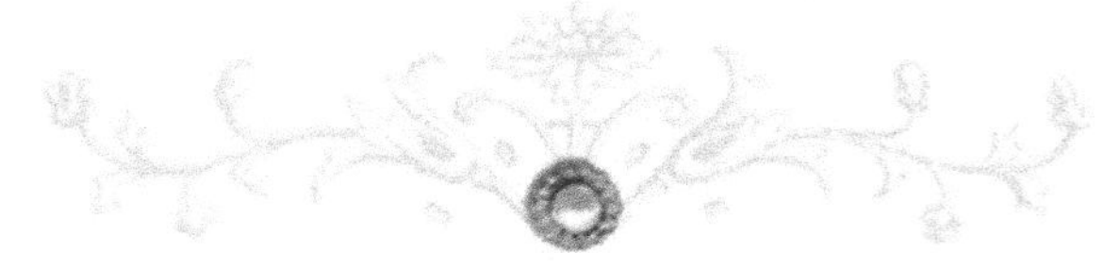

Beauty and the Beast part2 by N.R.Hart

It will get easier they said, forgetting
about you...
but they misunderstood about you and me
and the moon.
Because the purest love exists not only
in light but also in darkness;
and how you cannot have one without
the other.
I never feared your darkness
for I was in love with your moonlight;
it was your untamed strength
and how I became your weakness...
that lured me the most.
The wild beast lurking within the man
tamed only by the true love of his beauty.

-N.R.Hart ©

They say opposites attract
but we were too much alike
from the start
you were something
I understood...
sometimes, all too well.
Because understanding you
meant loving you
way too much.

Even more than I should.

-N.R.Hart "loving you"

Sometimes, she needs
him in ways even she
does not understand.
To be close to him
to lose herself inside
his rugged embrace
just to feel again.

-N.R.Hart "her"

I always knew we were different...
There is one true love story in your lifetime
that is unlike any other.
And, it will steal your soul for all eternity.
This kind of love feels different...
like nothing you have ever felt before or ever
will again. It was the most you have ever felt.
And, I never questioned how or why, because
loving you made me feel more like myself.
It went beyond all reason. It never made
sense. But, the greatest loves rarely do.
They just were and you lived them...
without trying to understand them.
It was a part of you. It was all of you. And,
it was different. And, we were different.
*"Because, even if I tried to explain us...they would
never understand."* -N.R.Hart

"we were different..."

And, my body collapsed into
yours and I didn't know how
two people could miss
each other more than this...
the longing the craving
the release...
the way our bodies fit
together perfectly.
Our bodies communicated
for us. It was everything
we could not say...
I felt it and I know
you did too...
it was the beautiful chaos
of love.

-N.R.Hart / "beautiful chaos"

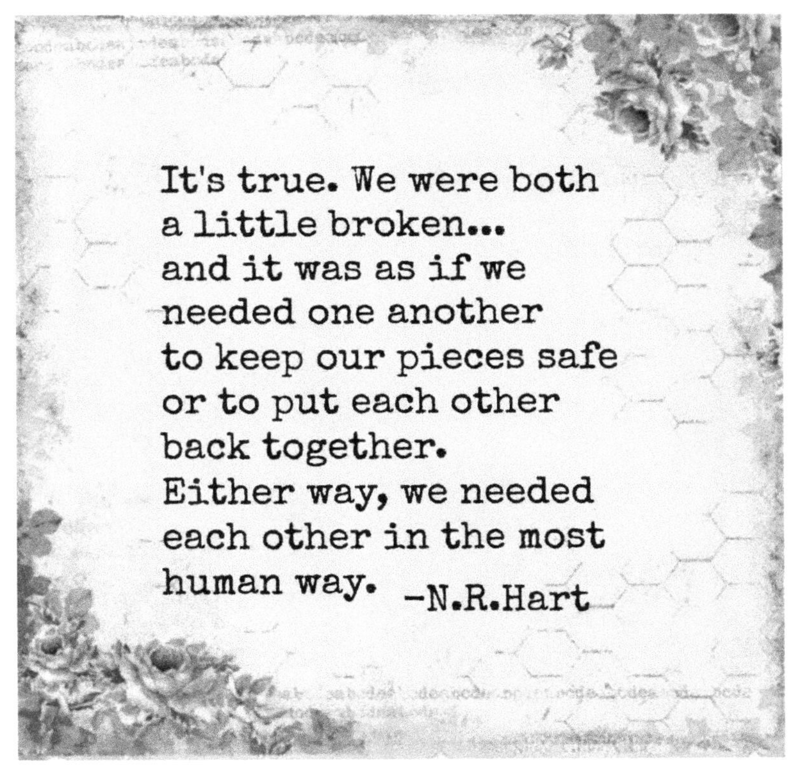
It's true. We were both
a little broken...
and it was as if we
needed one another
to keep our pieces safe
or to put each other
back together.
Either way, we needed
each other in the most
human way. -N.R.Hart

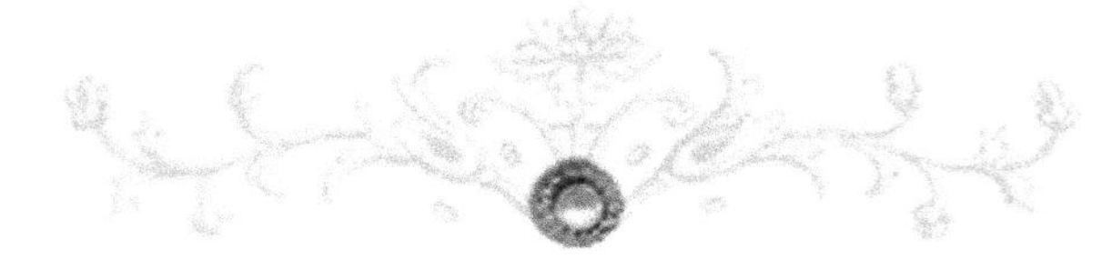

When love exists
on a soul level
it becomes
something else
entirely....
unfathomable, unbreakable
undeniable. Eternal.

-N.R.Hart

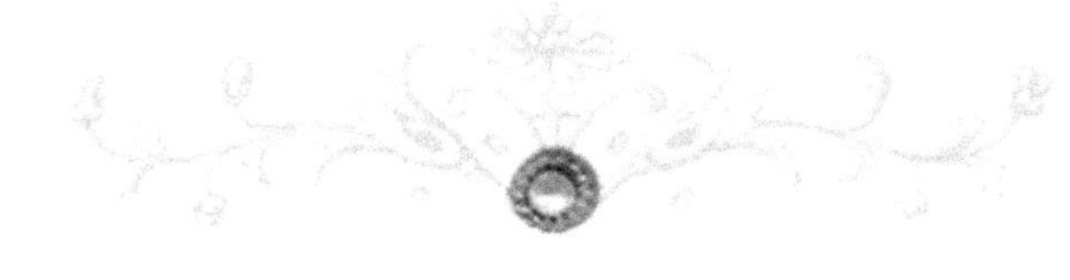

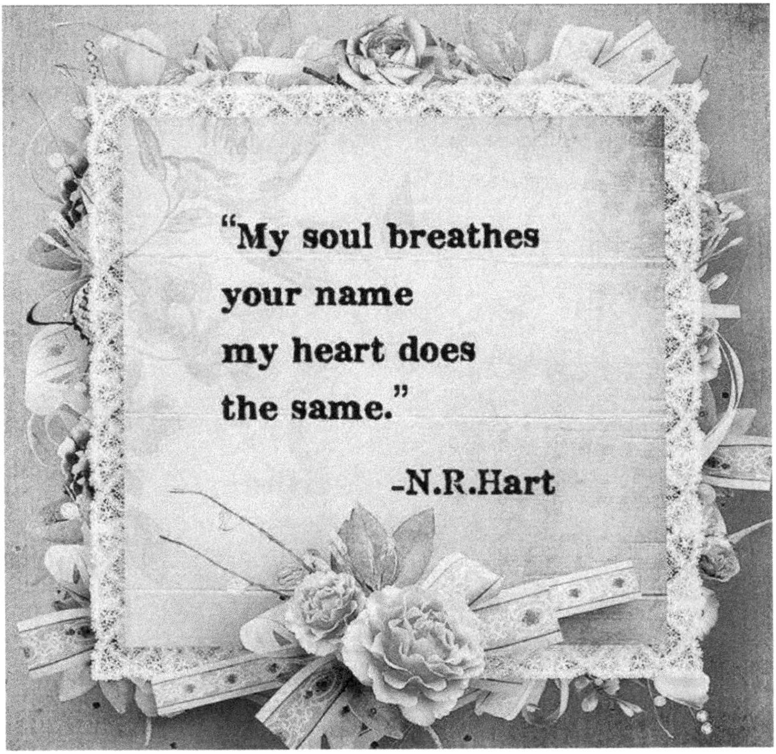

"My soul breathes
your name
my heart does
the same."

-N.R.Hart

I wouldn't use the word safe
in very many ways but I would
always use it for you...
I felt safe with you
the kind of safe that watches
over you, protecting you and I
would always find shelter in you.
Even when you are not here
I felt safe in my thoughts of you.
And this kind of safe feels
sacred to me.

-N.R.Hart "sacred"

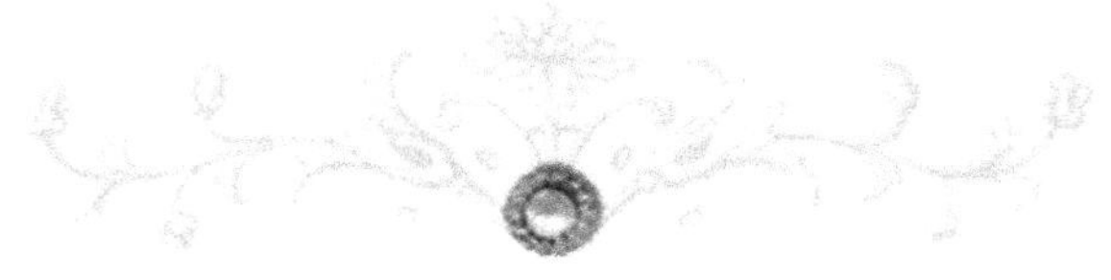

There are two sides
to every story
and maybe my side
is a bit more romantic
and a lot more poetic...
but in the end we both
spoke the same language
and god...we loved.
-N.R.Hart

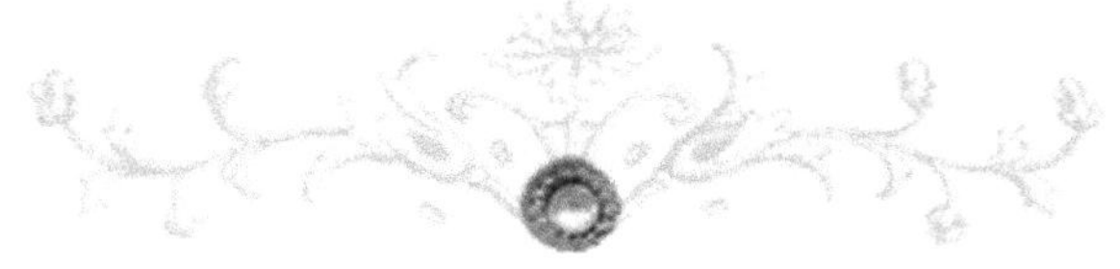

She wanted him.
He was her definition of desire.
She never knew how engulfing
the flames could be until now.
The only thing that could bring her
back to life...his lips, his hands.
She would follow him to the ends
of time just to have another moment
with him.
All she knew was she missed him
and nothing made sense until
she could be with him again.
This is what it felt like to fall
and not care where you land.

N.R.Hart / "land"

She felt something was different
about him the moment she laid eyes on him
and she thought to herself
he will be a dangerous one...
not only because their souls were
magically drawn to each other
beyond all reason but this powerful force
towards one another overtook her...
a complete surrendering of souls
and it scared her what she might do for him.
It was a chaotic love...a sweet creeping
madness between them like nothing she had
ever experienced before. And once you have
experienced euphoric passion...
there was no going back to ordinary love.
Maybe...just maybe...a consuming love
like that cannot last and her cruelest fate
she had a taste of something she couldn't
live without...yet was destined to.

N.R. Hart || a love like that

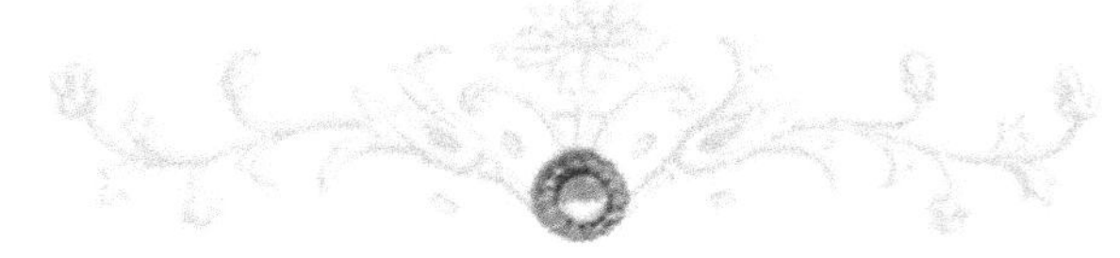

Whether fate stepped in
she only knew one thing
she was supposed to be
with him
a lover a friend
a secret or a sin. -N.R.Hart

"Fate"

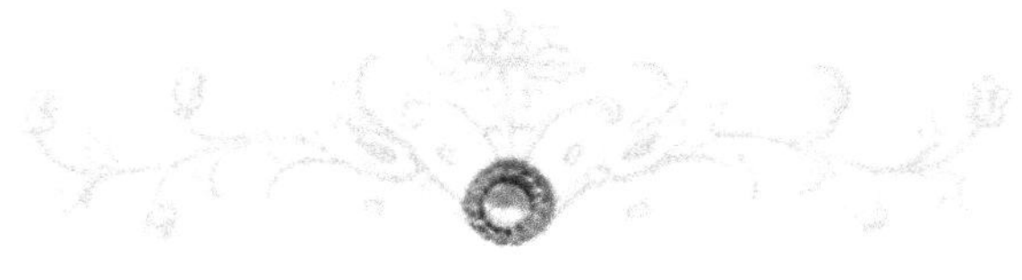

"She wants a
warrior lover...
with wild eyes
strong hands and
a poet's heart."

- N.R. Hart

I am your girl.
If you are stuck between here
or there or anywhere
I will move mountains for you
if it is the darkness you fear
I will sit there with you
if you need to be kissed
I will set us both on fire
if you need an escape
from this life I will drive
the get-away car.
I have always been right here
waiting...
I have always been your girl
and I love you. Let's go.

-N.R.Hart "your girl"

And, it had been a long while
since we saw each other last.
You held me tight not letting go
and I felt our souls pass through
one another...
Your familiar hands finding
their way to my bare skin
demanding me to feel you again,
to love you again...
I was breathless when you took me
as our bodies became one
a hunger so strong it felt as though
we had been starving, until now
and we were holding our breath,
until now...
and the earth hadn't moved at all,
until now.
And, we were barely breathing at all,
until now. -N.R.Hart (until now)

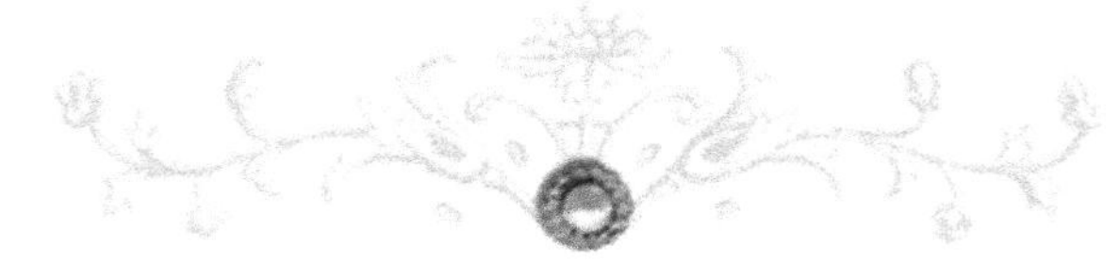

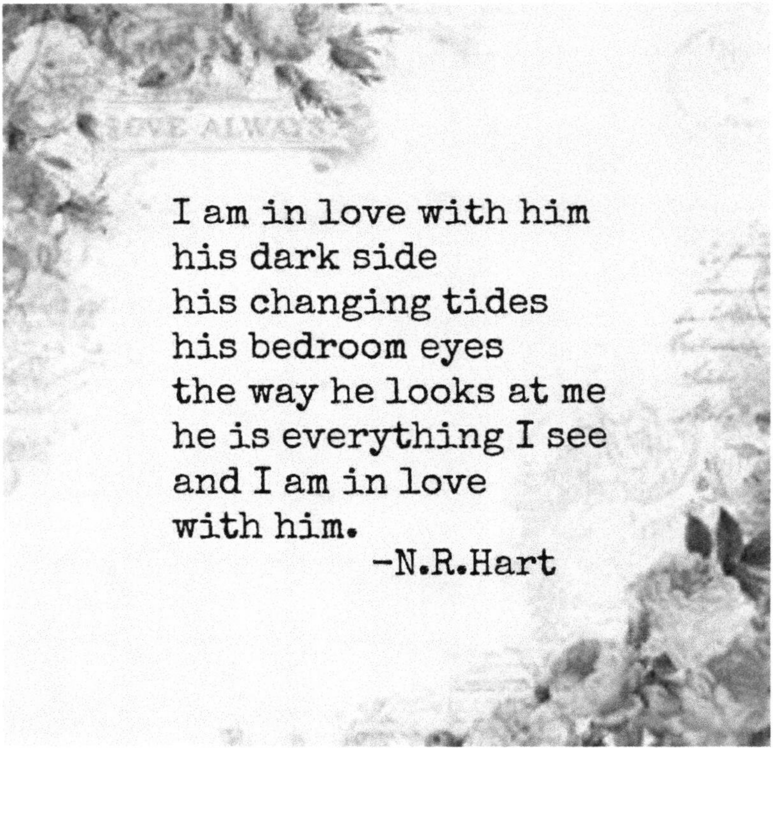

I am in love with him
his dark side
his changing tides
his bedroom eyes
the way he looks at me
he is everything I see
and I am in love
with him.

-N.R.Hart

It's true. We never made
any promises to each other.
But, god I would somehow disagree
with that statement now.
Your hands, they made promises
worshipping my body
your voice, all the words you never said
sit inside my throat, whispering
sweet dirty nothings
your staring eyes chanting
promises into mine.
And even though they were unutterable,
these promises...
I still feel them living inside us
like something holy.
Something like a prayer. -N.R.Hart

I don't know if he felt it
first or me
we looked at each other
differently that day
the universe nodded
in agreement
a long awaited kiss...
that was always meant to be
the stars aligned perfectly
our lips struck like lightning
a blazing kiss...jolting us
back to life that day.

N.R.Hart 28/4/10

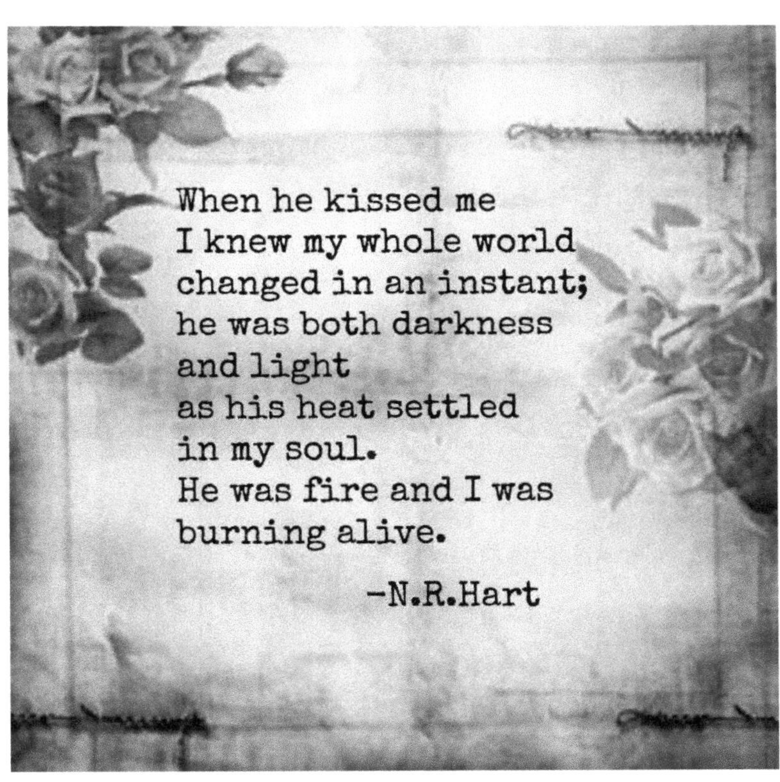
When he kissed me
I knew my whole world
changed in an instant;
he was both darkness
and light
as his heat settled
in my soul.
He was fire and I was
burning alive.
-N.R.Hart

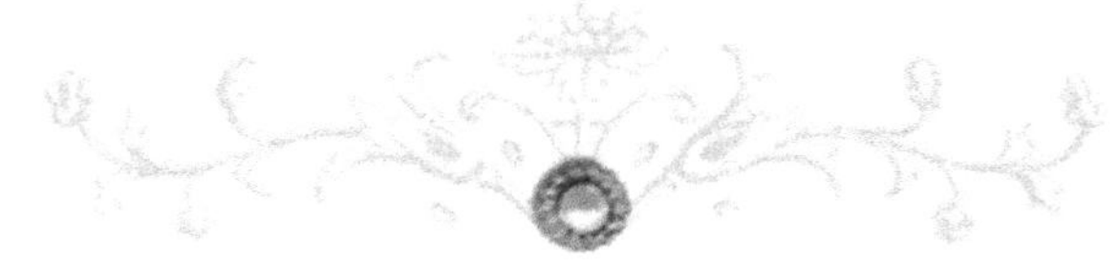

"Love"

While I do believe in having an attraction like chemistry with love...and things like pheromones, but that is as scientic as I get when it comes to understanding love.
I am more of a romantic and do not believe love to be a science at all.
But, it is more of a phenomenon we have some trouble understanding.
Love is big and vast and made of far more mysterious things...things like feelings... that cannot be easily explained. The ones there are no words for.
The hard words, the impossible words, the ones that get stuck in your throat because the feelings overtake you.
I believe in those things...like love... that are much bigger than us. The things we do not understand, yet we believe in them, simply because we feel them. Things like the universe, souls and the stars. -N.R.Hart

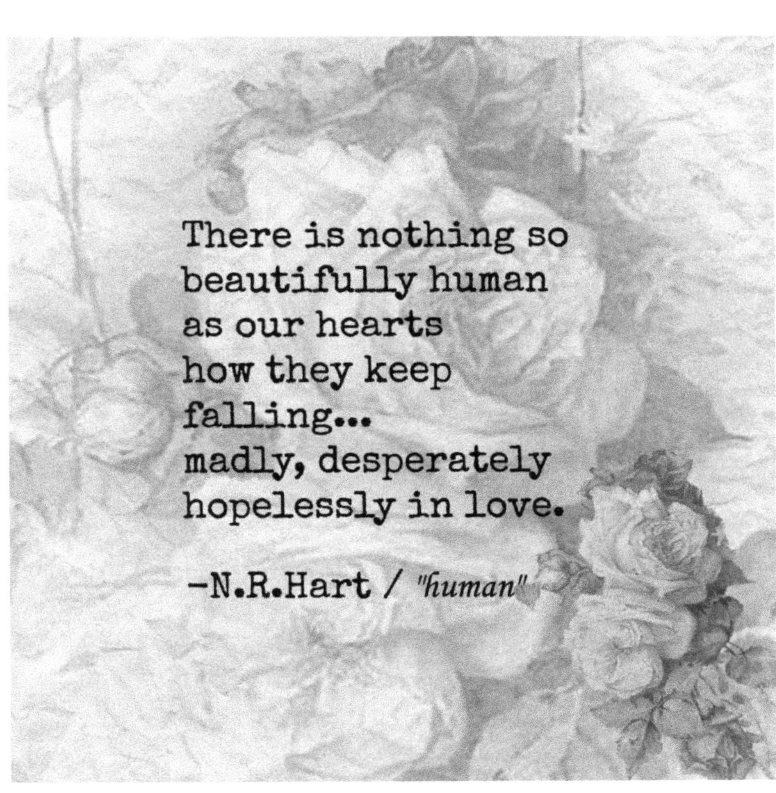
There is nothing so
beautifully human
as our hearts
how they keep
falling...
madly, desperately
hopelessly in love.
-N.R.Hart / "human"

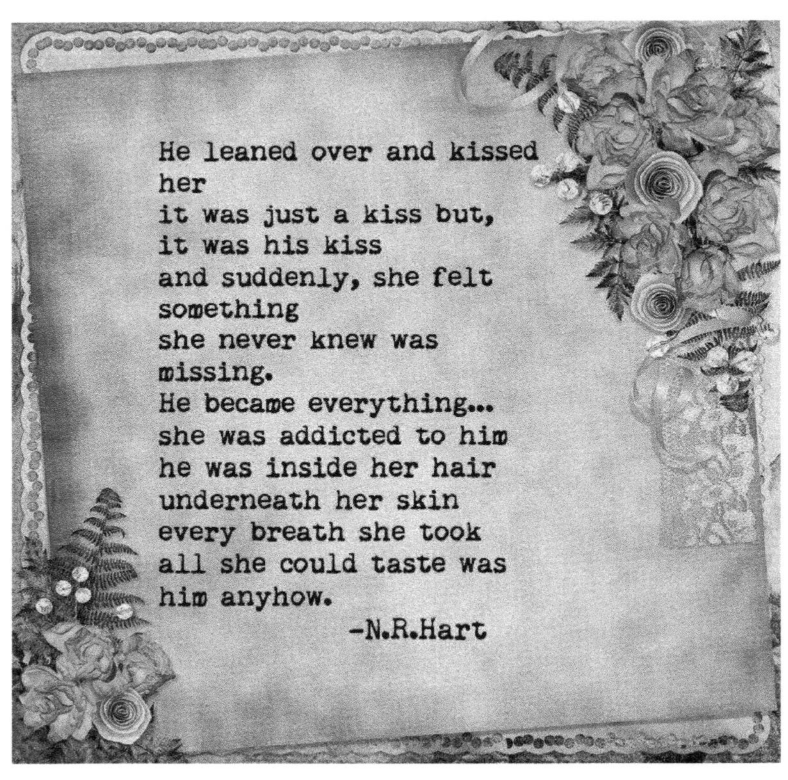
He leaned over and kissed
her
it was just a kiss but,
it was his kiss
and suddenly, she felt
something
she never knew was
missing.
He became everything...
she was addicted to him
he was inside her hair
underneath her skin
every breath she took
all she could taste was
him anyhow.
-N.R.Hart

He is unaware of his affect on her. With his words
he transports her into his world where only they exist.
And, even though they are worlds apart, their words
crush each other like skin on skin allowing them to feel
each other, touch each other's bodies.
She could feel his eyes raking over her, his hands
crawling underneath her skin, peeling away her petals
exposing her soul. With his words breathing life
back into her, a sweetness so thicke and lingering
her lungs were full of his scent. She fell into him
like she fell into his eyes, losing herself completely
in the feel of him. He controlled her mind as his words
melted their bodies into one. She was helpless, her heart
fluttering in the breeze, dying to be captured by the
mighty sails in his strong embrace. He devoured her
like a work of art, stroking her with each word,
learning her...inside and out. She felt known by him and
never felt so precious in his love. N.R.Hart "precious"

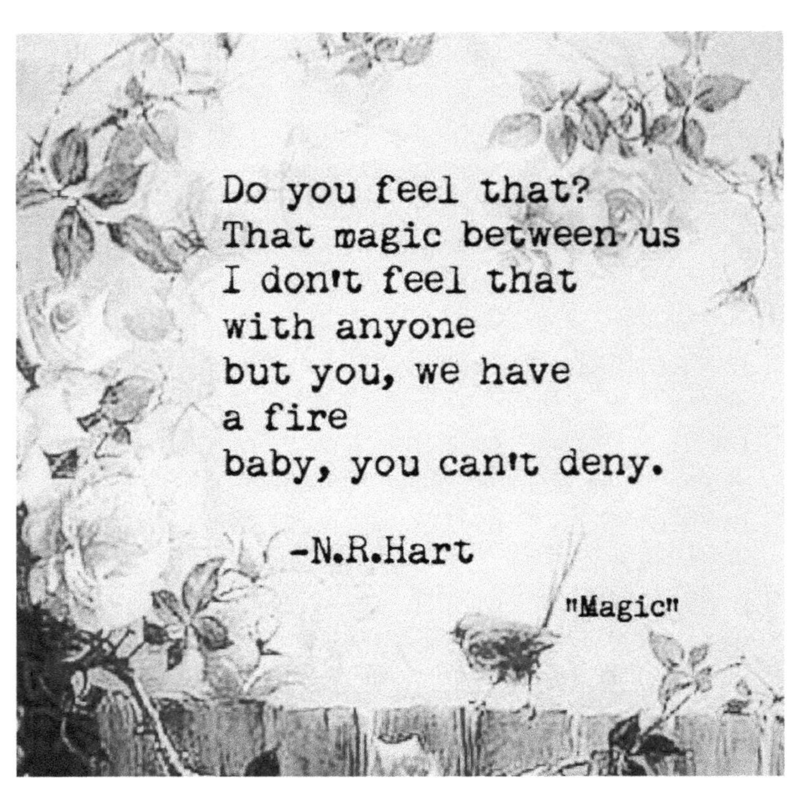
Do you feel that?
That magic between us
I don't feel that
with anyone
but you, we have
a fire
baby, you can't deny.
-N.R.Hart
"Magic"

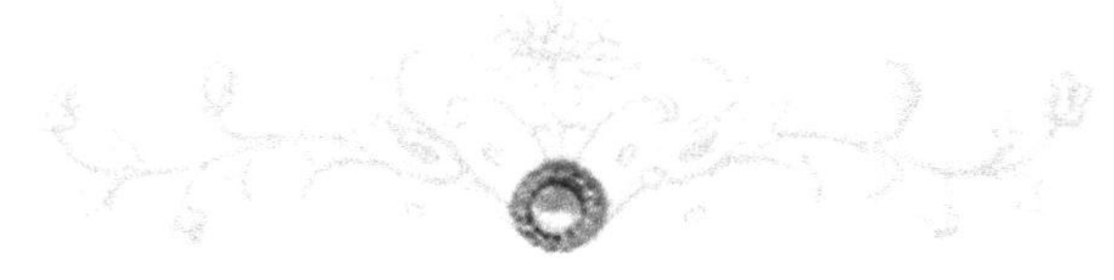

Twin Flames

It was as if they were connected on a
different plane from everything else;
and it was the two of them in their own
little world.
How they had a secret language between souls
and their fiery energy fed off each other.
They didn't always need words because
they could communicate through silence.
They had each other memorized and they
could feel one another through time
and space.
Their souls were always touching
like twin flames, existing within each other
and burning through everything else.

They were only certain of one thing.
It felt right to be with one another.

—N.R.Hart *"twin flames"*

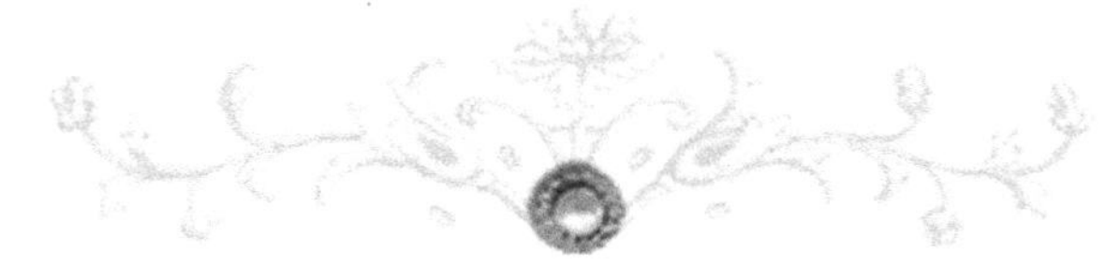

We were soul deep
in love
our souls loved
one another
long before we ever knew
this was a once
in a lifetime love.
One we cannot undo.
-N.R.Hart

She sat next to him in the passenger
seat looking out the window...with
so many thoughts racing through
her head. She could never tell him
though...it would probably scare him.
His heart had been broken before...
and badly...she saw his scars.
All of them.
So she kept her feelings to herself
when all she could think of was how
much she loved being with him. She
felt the entire universe with him
and all she wanted was to show him
so he could feel love again.
With every part of her on fire she kept
staring out the window...quietly
burning and hoping...that somehow,
he was feeling it too.

-N.R.Hart "love, her perspective"

And, then one day she stopped
trying to fit into a world
others had created for her
and she decided to create
her own.
She wanted it all...
the romance of life
the devastation of love.
She wanted to 'feel' her life
while she was living it.
She did not want to get to
the end of her life not loving
what she was meant to love.
-N.R.Hart

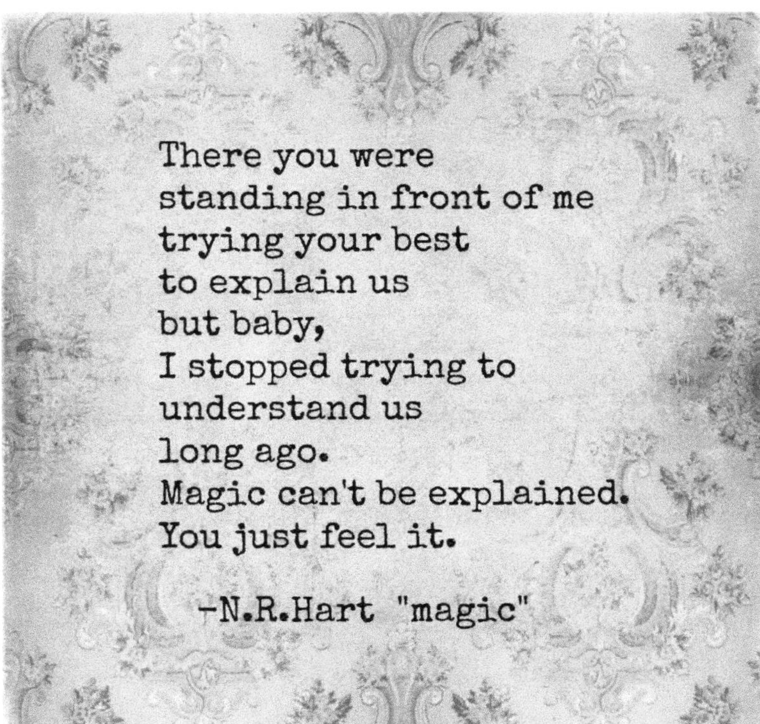
There you were
standing in front of me
trying your best
to explain us
but baby,
I stopped trying to
understand us
long ago.
Magic can't be explained.
You just feel it.
-N.R.Hart "magic"

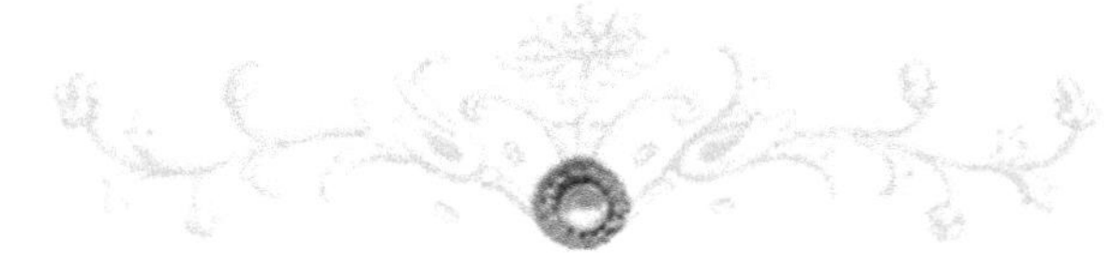

Look into her eyes
grab a fistful of her hair
pull her mouth towards yours
and kiss her
kiss her hard then softer
kiss her deeply
until you can taste her soul
kiss her like you mean it
kiss her...
like it's agony not to.

-N.R.Hart "kiss her"

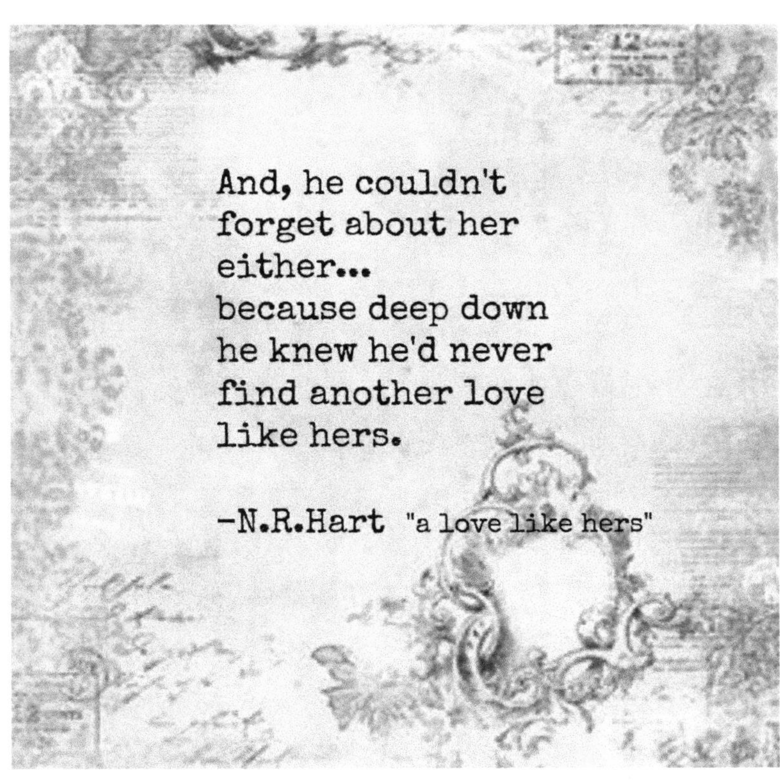
And, he couldn't
forget about her
either...
because deep down
he knew he'd never
find another love
like hers.

-N.R.Hart "a love like hers"

The space between us feels
far away now and the silence
so very loud
these hollow heartbeats
with tender words left unsaid
and little worlds fall away
dangling over the edge
ready to jump or fall
as I desperately search
for a sign...any sign
that you are looking for me too.

-N.R.Hart / "little worlds"

"More"

She will always want more.
You have awakened the sleeping parts
in her heating her blood to boiling.
She breathes differently now.
Deeper. Fuller. Harder.
You are a powerful gust of wind
filling her fully with your fragrance.
She is alive now. Passion consumes her.
So do you. It will never be enough.
And, she never knew she was starving
until she tasted your kind of love.
A love that makes you feel so alive
and kills you all at once...when
you are without it.
You see, love will bleed you dry.
You just have to pick the ones
worth dying for. -N.R.Hart

I like you.
And, not in a normal way
but in a breathless
sort of way.
Not in a fluttering
of butterflies way
but in a scary heart-pounding
kind of way.
Not in I want to get to know you
but in I want you in a desperate
human sort of way.

I like you that way.

-N.R.Hart "I like you that way"

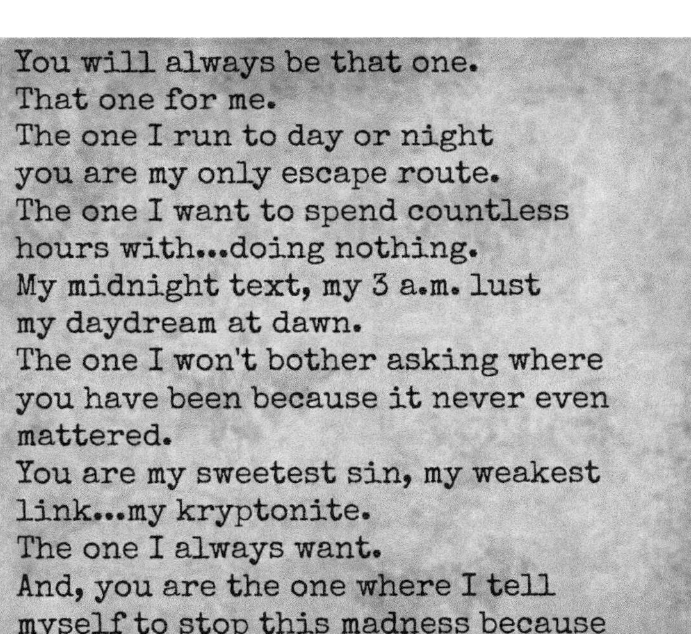
You will always be that one.
That one for me.
The one I run to day or night
you are my only escape route.
The one I want to spend countless
hours with...doing nothing.
My midnight text, my 3 a.m. lust
my daydream at dawn.
The one I won't bother asking where
you have been because it never even
mattered.
You are my sweetest sin, my weakest
link...my kryptonite.
The one I always want.
And, you are the one where I tell
myself to stop this madness because
after all, enough is enough.
But, it never is. Never. -N.R.Hart
"my kryptonite"

She was a sweet chaos
hiding behind a delicate
soul and a vulnerable smile.
She loves like the rage
of a storm the heat of a
wildfire...
and looking into her eyes
she always reminds you
what it's like to feel alive.

-N.R.Hart "sweet chaos"

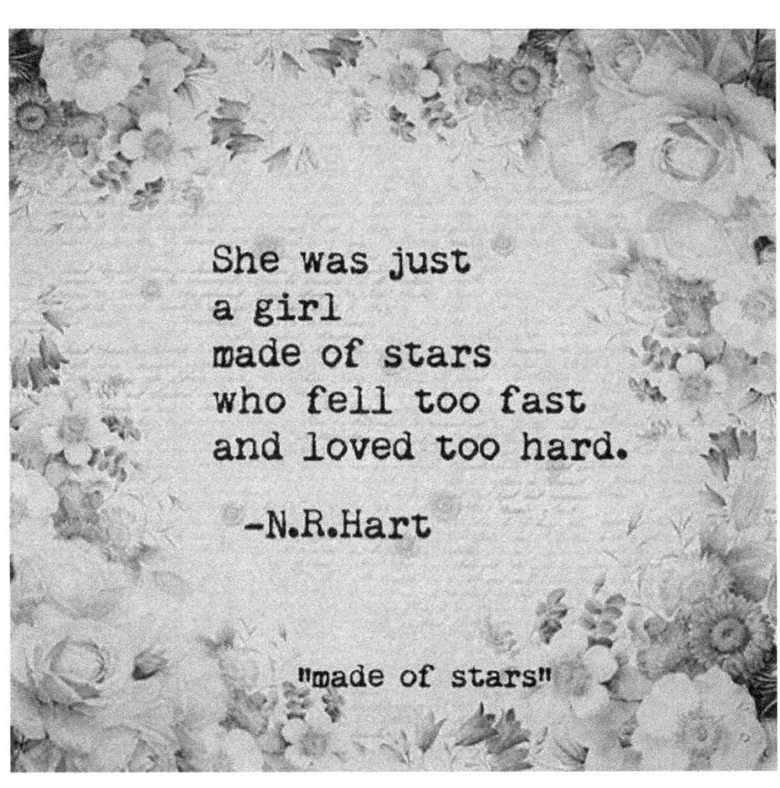
She was just
a girl
made of stars
who fell too fast
and loved too hard.
-N.R.Hart
"made of stars"

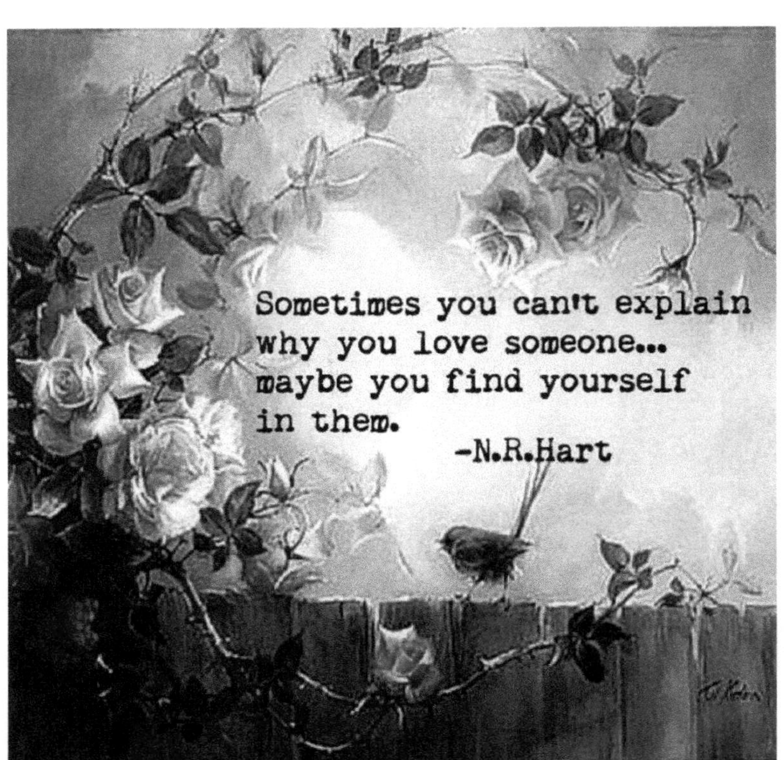
Sometimes you can't explain
why you love someone...
maybe you find yourself
in them.
-N.R.Hart

"I did it for love"
And, if you were to
ask me
why I did it
why I do everything...
Well, the answer is simple,
I did it for love.
-N.R.Hart

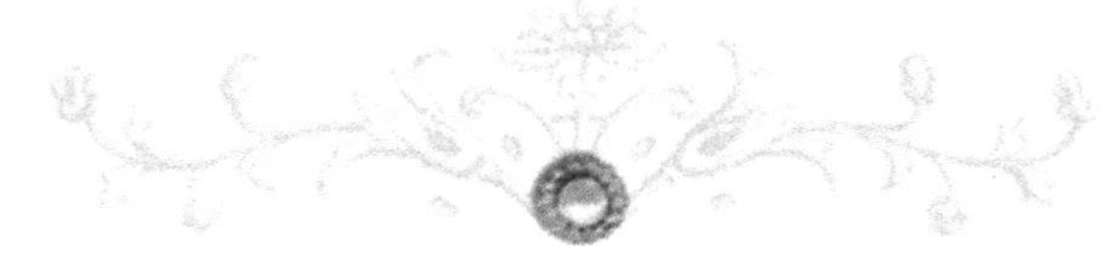

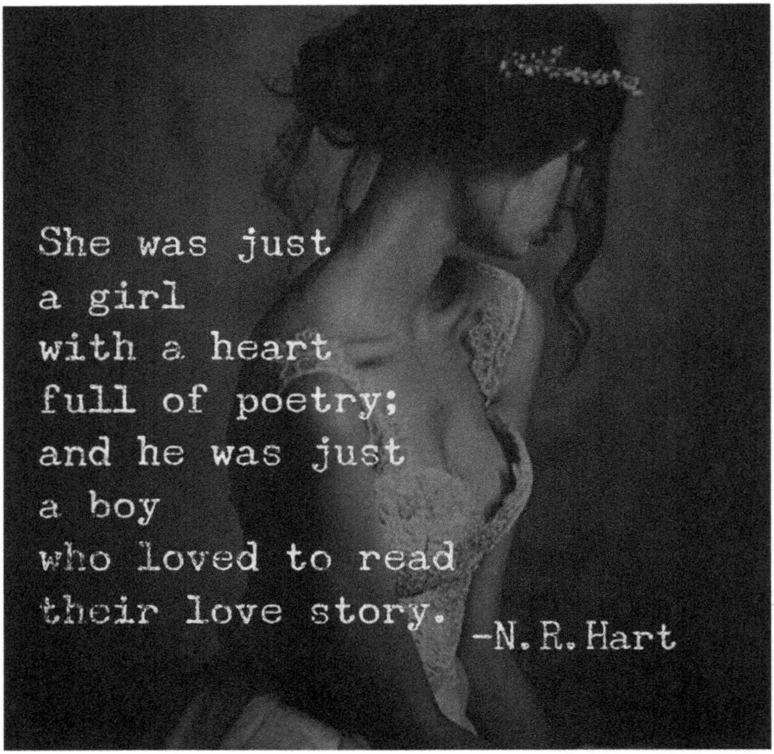

She was just
a girl
with a heart
full of poetry;
and he was just
a boy
who loved to read
their love story.
-N.R.Hart

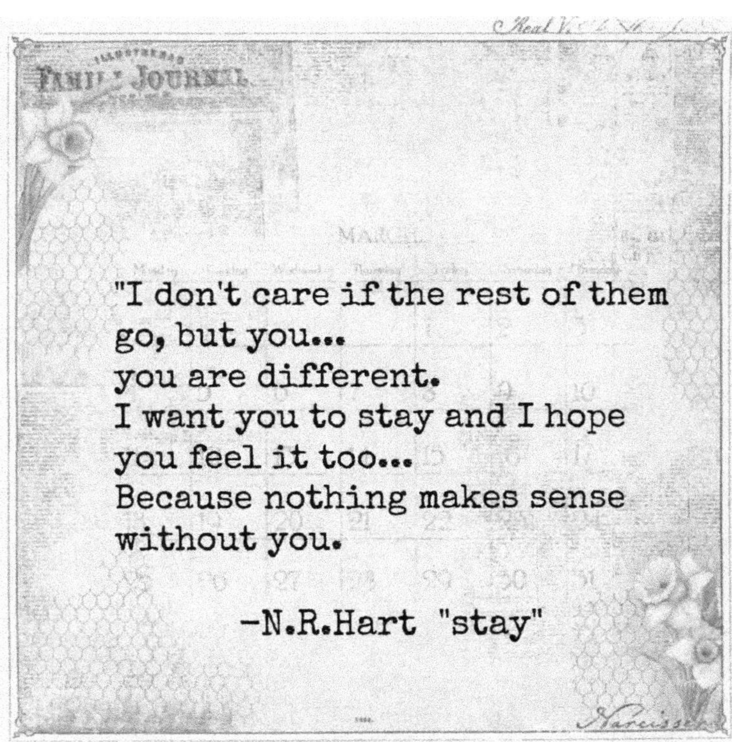
"I don't care if the rest of them
go, but you...
you are different.
I want you to stay and I hope
you feel it too...
Because nothing makes sense
without you.
-N.R.Hart "stay"

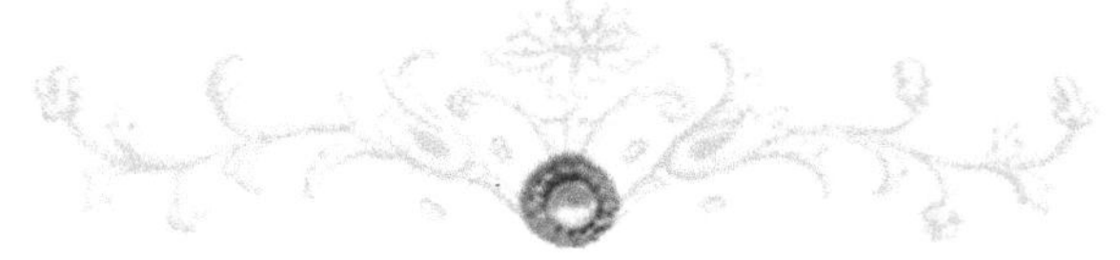

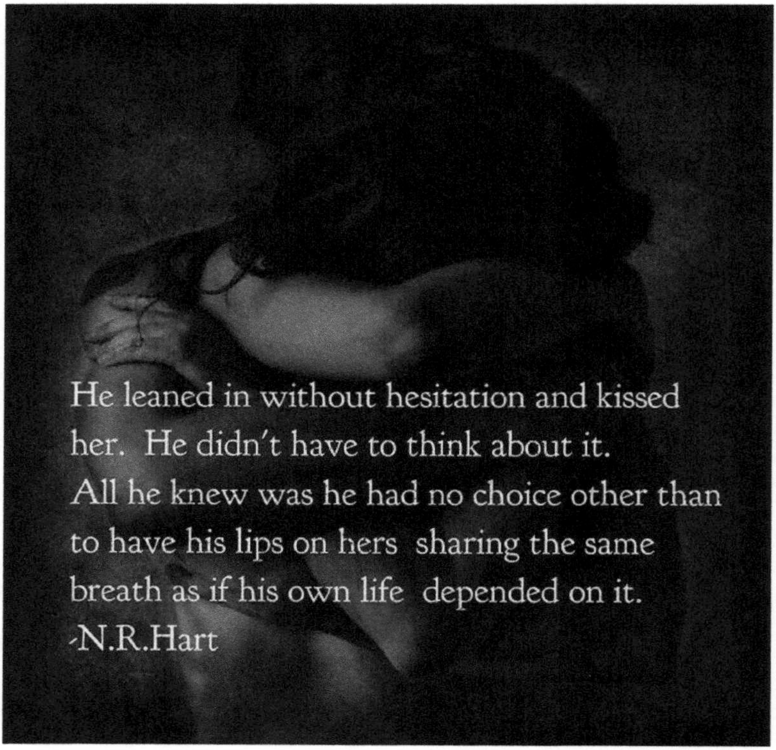

He leaned in without hesitation and kissed her. He didn't have to think about it. All he knew was he had no choice other than to have his lips on hers sharing the same breath as if his own life depended on it.
-N.R.Hart

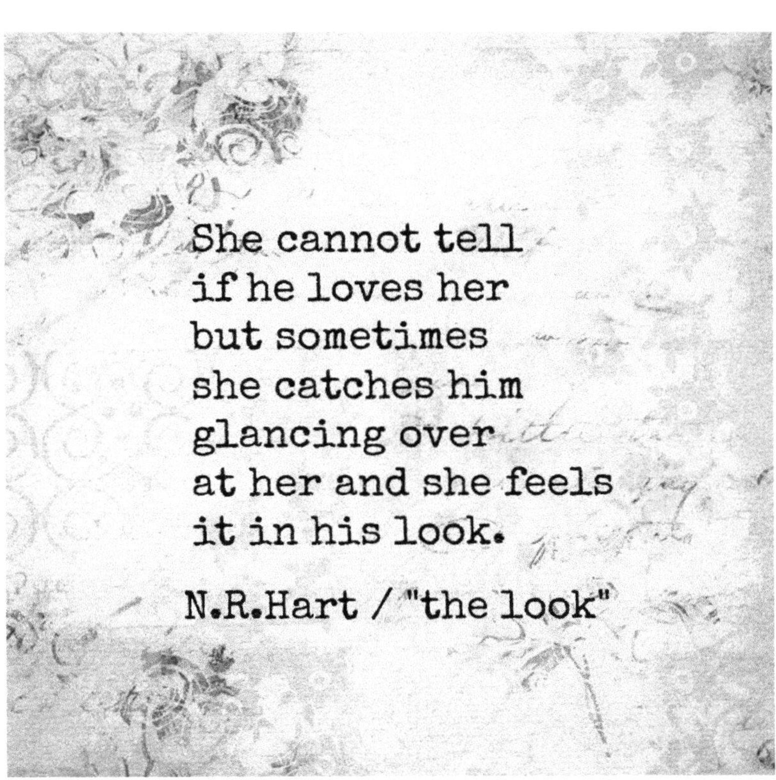
She cannot tell
if he loves her
but sometimes
she catches him
glancing over
at her and she feels
it in his look.
N.R.Hart / "the look"

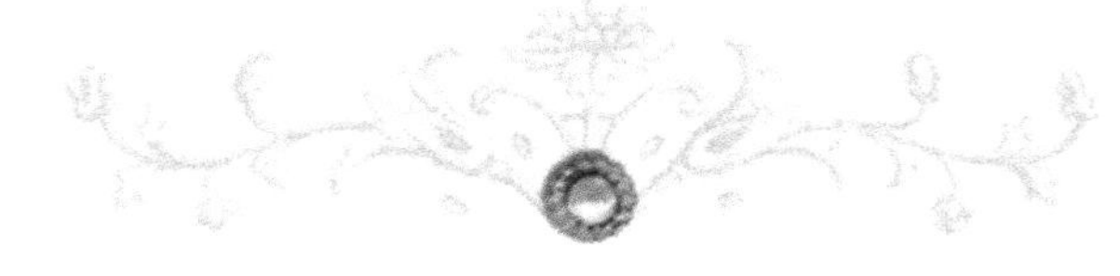

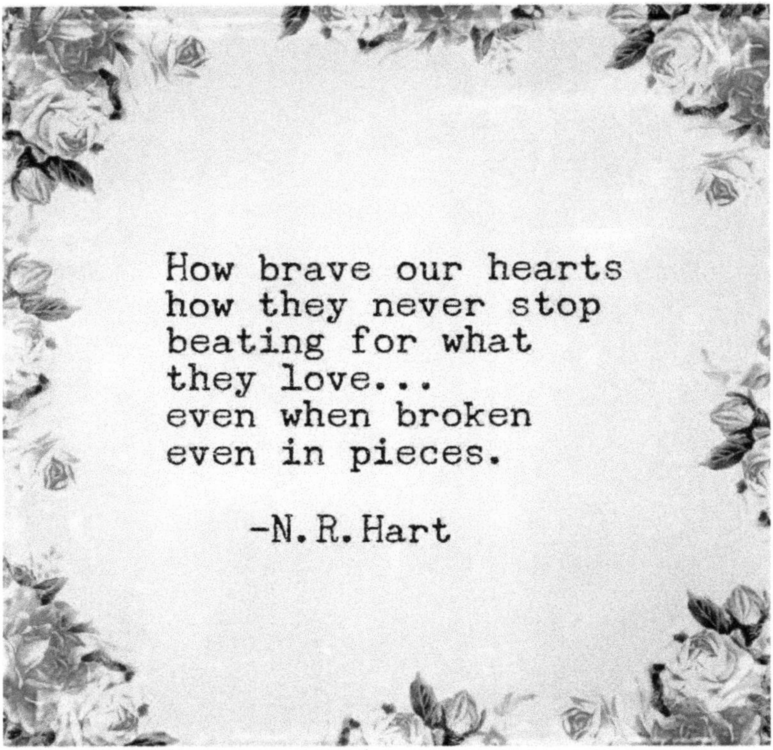

How brave our hearts
how they never stop
beating for what
they love...
even when broken
even in pieces.

-N.R.Hart

LOVE AT FIRST SIGHT

When they asked her
why she loved him
her answer was
always the same...
she loved him from
the first moment
they met...
and it had always
been so.

- N.R. Hart

Pillow talk

You don't know this, but
sometimes I think of you
at midnight...
when the night is still
the silence speaks to us.
I have learned that
darkness never lies.
It tells us what we fear
losing...
one of them is always you.

-N.R.Hart

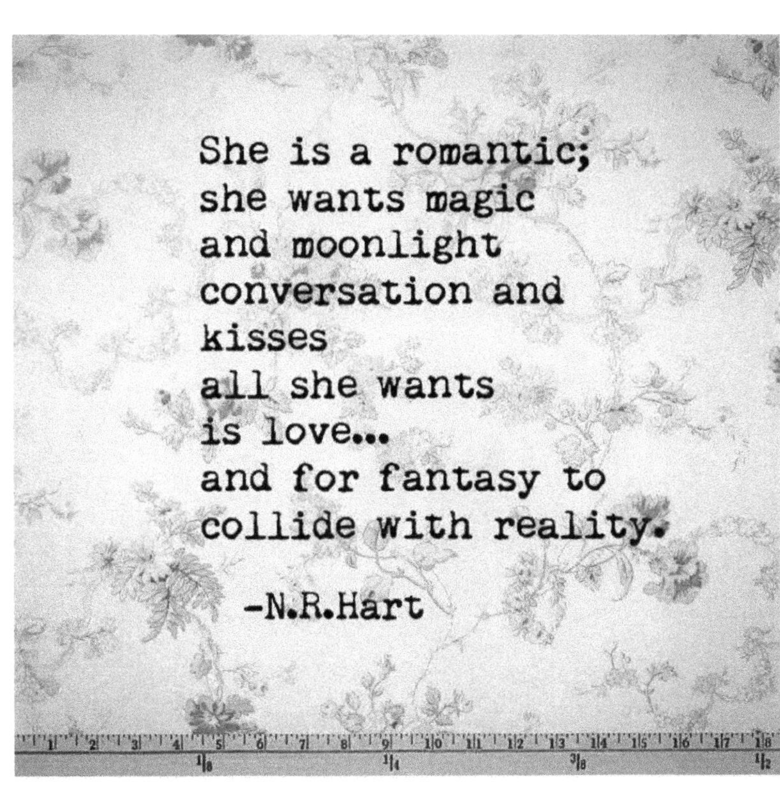
She is a romantic;
she wants magic
and moonlight
conversation and
kisses
all she wants
is love...
and for fantasy to
collide with reality.
-N.R.Hart

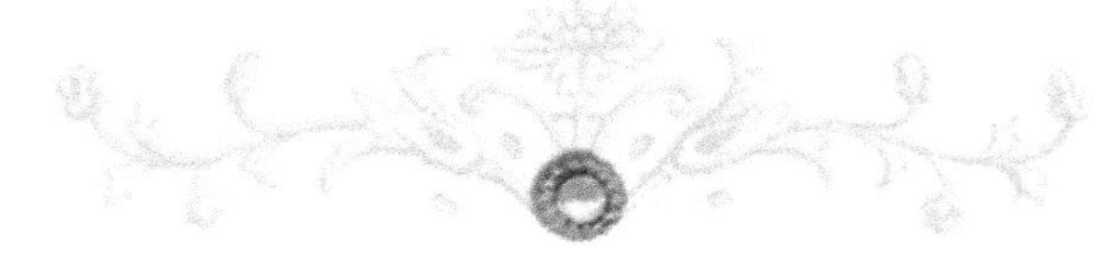

A deep hunger...
as our souls sank
into one another
and with one hard
thrust; he took me
all of me...
I wanted to be
taken.
I wanted to be his.

-N.R.Hart

She is springtime
sweet blushing hyacinths and
dew-kissed meadows
warm honeyed days and soft
mossy nights.
She is the violet sun.
He is summer
dusky twilights and dreamy
midnights
tangled in stars and darkness
and heat.
He is the sapphire moon.

-N.R.Hart "spring&summer"

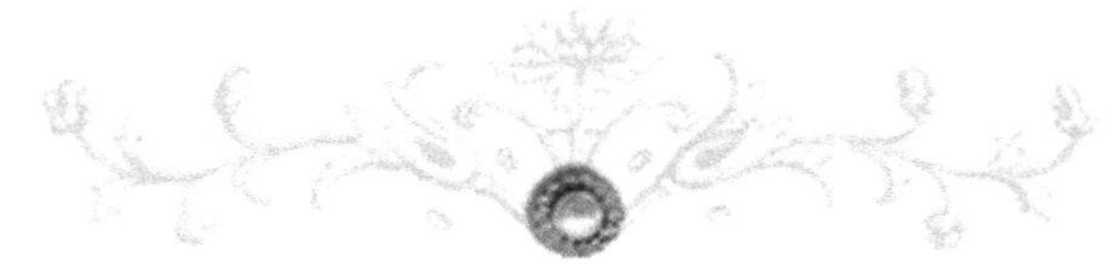

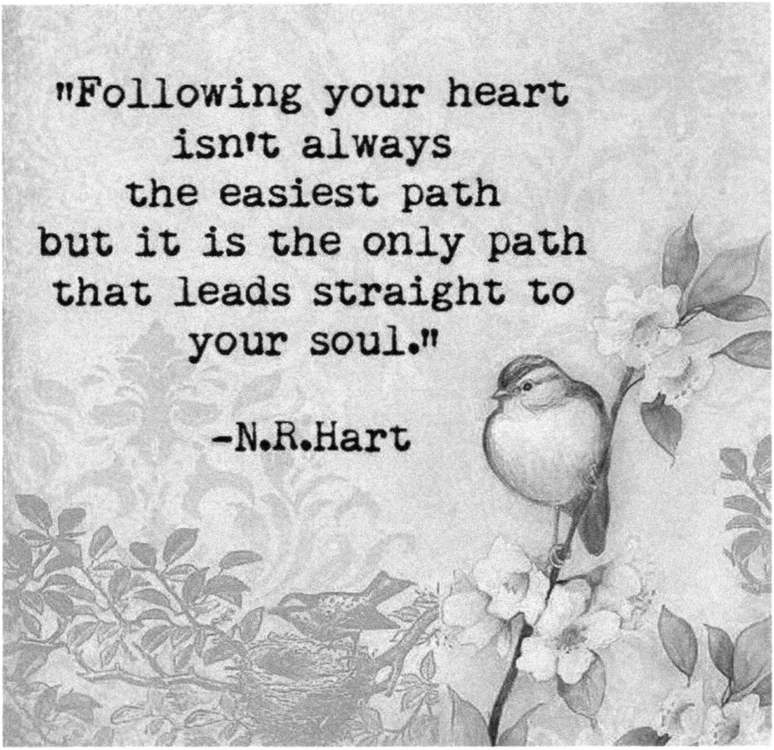

"Following your heart
isn't always
the easiest path
but it is the only path
that leads straight to
your soul."

-N.R.Hart

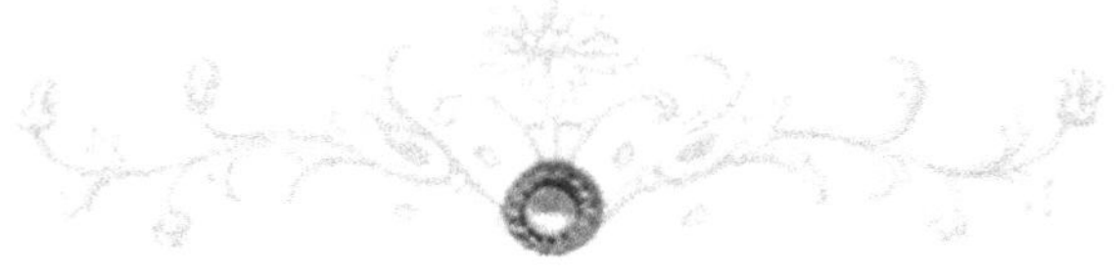

A Summer Season

"This wild heart of mine is

just too much sometimes."

N.R.Hart

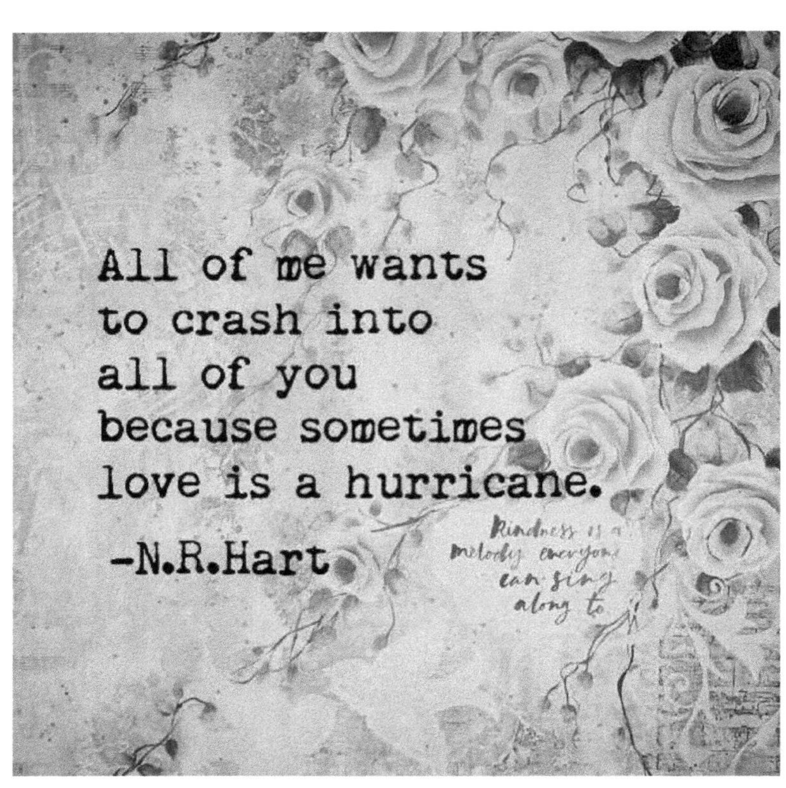
All of me wants
to crash into
all of you
because sometimes
love is a hurricane.
-N.R.Hart
Kindness is a
melody everyone
can sing
along to

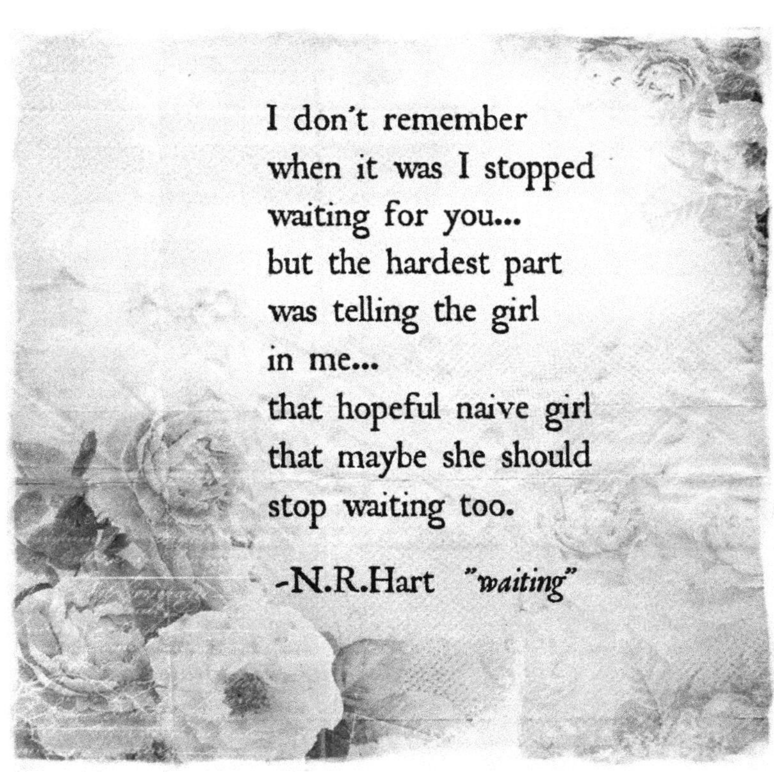
I don't remember
when it was I stopped
waiting for you...
but the hardest part
was telling the girl
in me...
that hopeful naive girl
that maybe she should
stop waiting too.
-N.R.Hart "waiting"

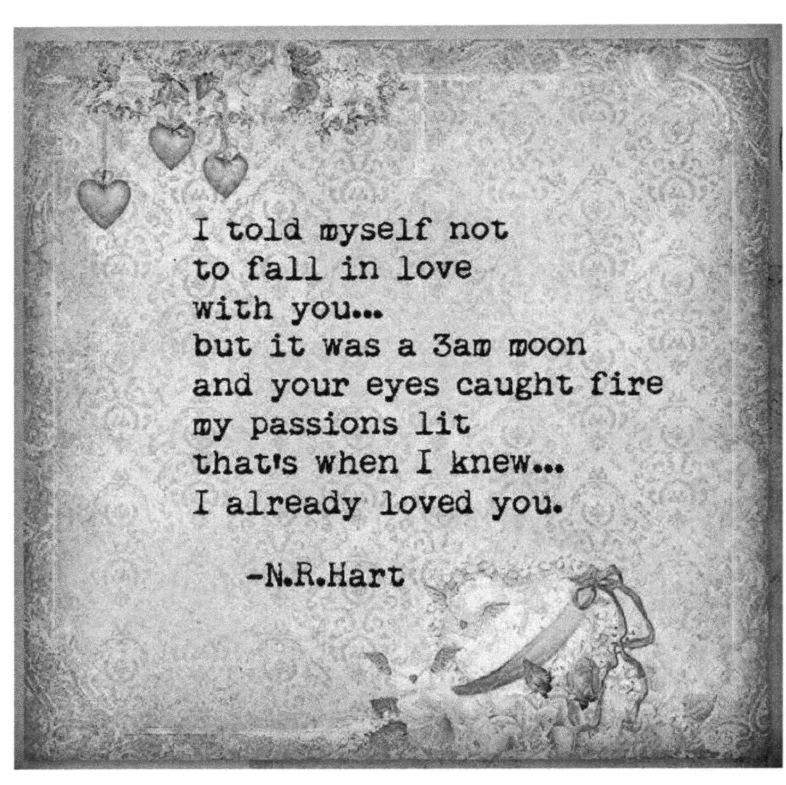
I told myself not
to fall in love
with you...
but it was a 3am moon
and your eyes caught fire
my passions lit
that's when I knew...
I already loved you.

-N.R.Hart

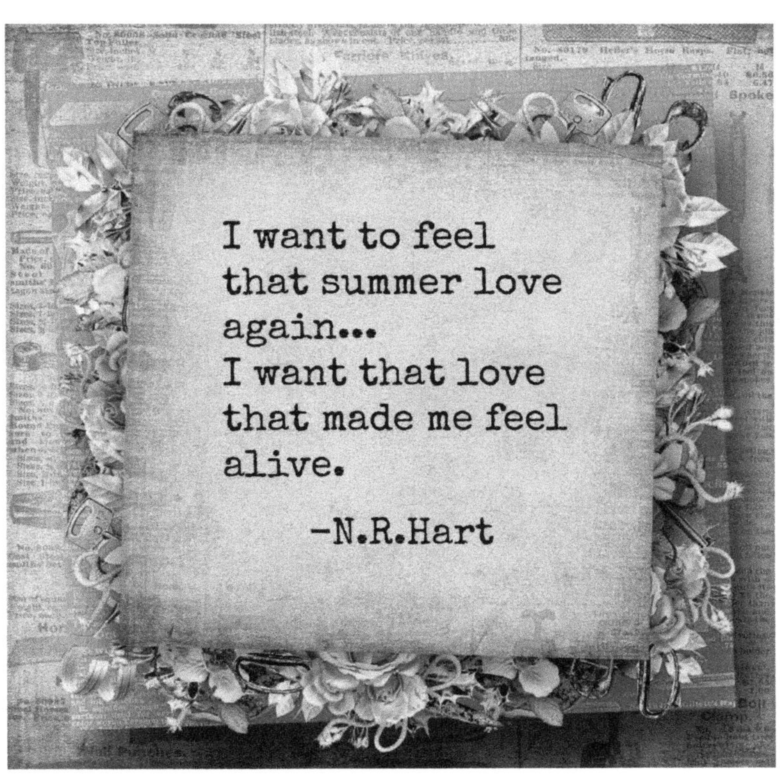
I want to feel
that summer love
again...
I want that love
that made me feel
alive.
-N.R.Hart

She is in love
with the moon
but she is made
from the sun;
she is fire
with a need to
burn.
-N.R.Hart
sun & moon

I still believe
in fairytales
and soulmates
and love...
and everything
that is magic.
N.R.HART

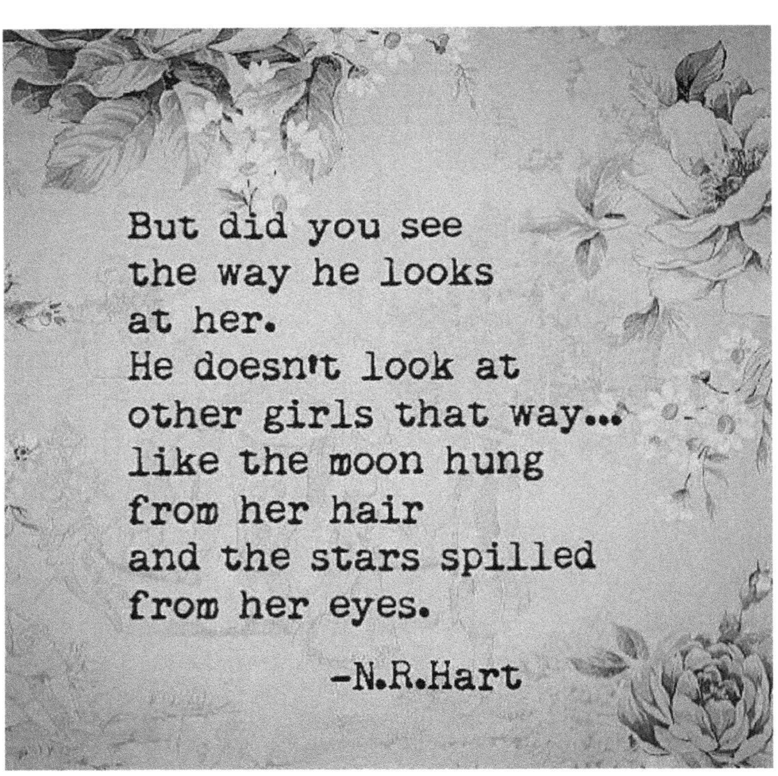
But did you see
the way he looks
at her.
He doesn't look at
other girls that way...
like the moon hung
from her hair
and the stars spilled
from her eyes.
-N.R.Hart

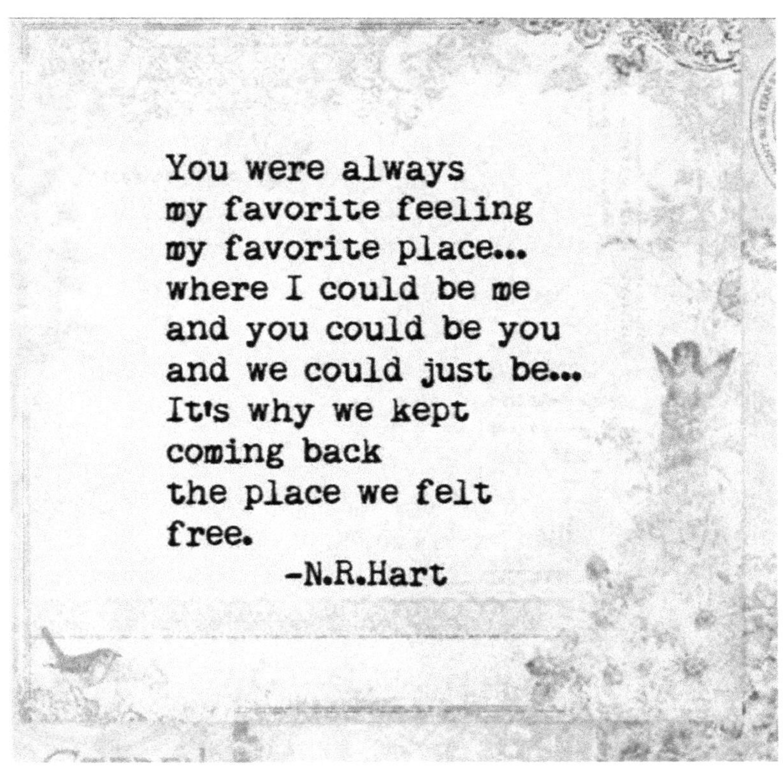
You were always
my favorite feeling
my favorite place...
where I could be me
and you could be you
and we could just be...
It's why we kept
coming back
the place we felt
free.
-N.R.Hart

Come Here

He said the words "come here" to her
and she didn't know what had come over her
hearing those two words they sounded
innocent enough but had the exact opposite
affect on her...bringing about images of
blood and fire the heat rushing to her head,
her skin burning her body electrified...
she suddenly felt lightheaded, dizzy
as if about to faint or maybe die...she wasn't
entirely certain which would come first ...
causing her to be fixated on one thought only,
please...let him come and take her now.

N.R. Hart

Interesting Stories

Sometimes, he needs
her in ways even he
does not understand.
To be close to her
to lose himself inside
her softness
just to feel again.
-N.R.Hart "him"

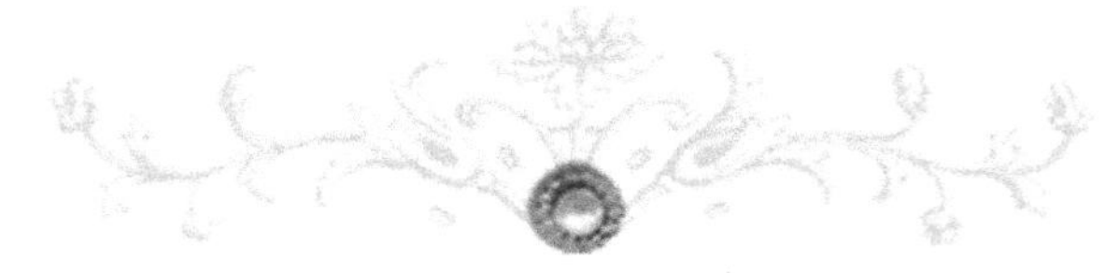

She is his dark fairytale
he is her wicked romance
novel
and their love story is what
legends are made of...
A pure friendship, a real romance
the best of both worlds
laughter and kisses
the fervor of passion
with bite marks and bruised lips
holding hands and fingerprints
pressed against flesh
the thrill of being alive...
Their souls stained with eternity
and sweet poetry. -N. R. Hart

"Legends"

I think we were burning
stars you and I....
lovers that were always
meant to find each other
no matter how many times
the world came between us
we kept finding
our way back
a cosmic pull
of the universe and just
like shooting stardust
we will continue to melt
and crash into each other
until the end of time.
-N.R.Hart

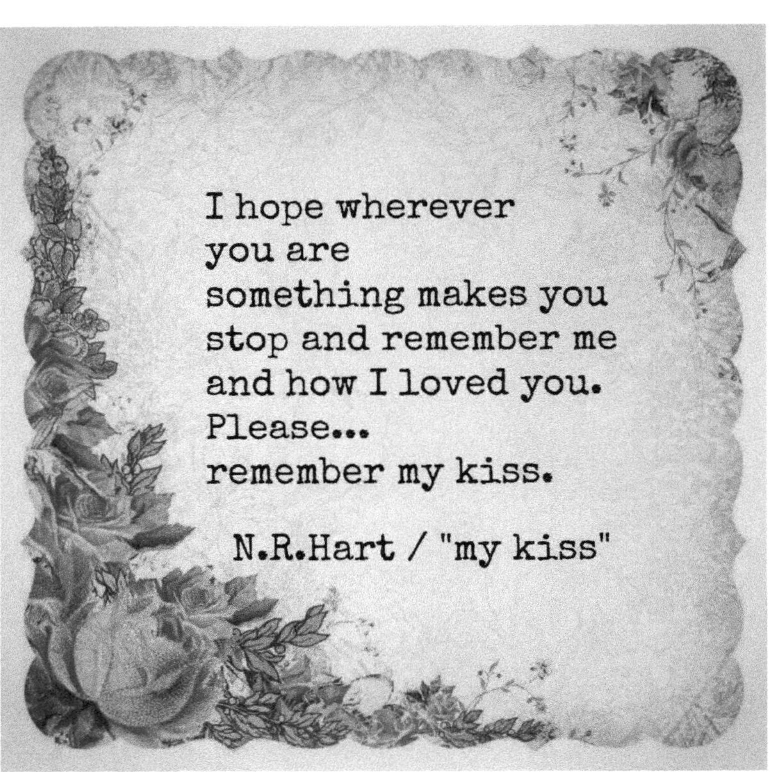
I hope wherever
you are
something makes you
stop and remember me
and how I loved you.
Please...
remember my kiss.
N.R.Hart / "my kiss"

Star-crossed lovers part2

Are we just star-crossed
lovers
revolving around each other
like drifting galaxies
shooting stars
reaching and missing
hoping and wishing
on one another...
aching to love in every
Universe
living for the day
our worlds finally collide.

-N.R.Hart

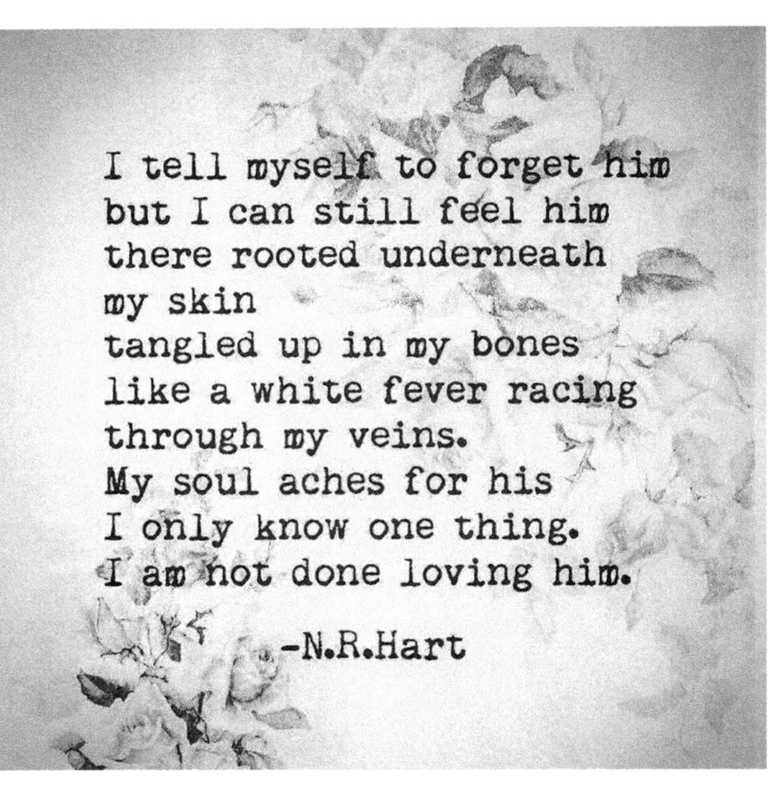
I tell myself to forget him
but I can still feel him
there rooted underneath
my skin
tangled up in my bones
like a white fever racing
through my veins.
My soul aches for his
I only know one thing.
I am not done loving him.
-N.R.Hart

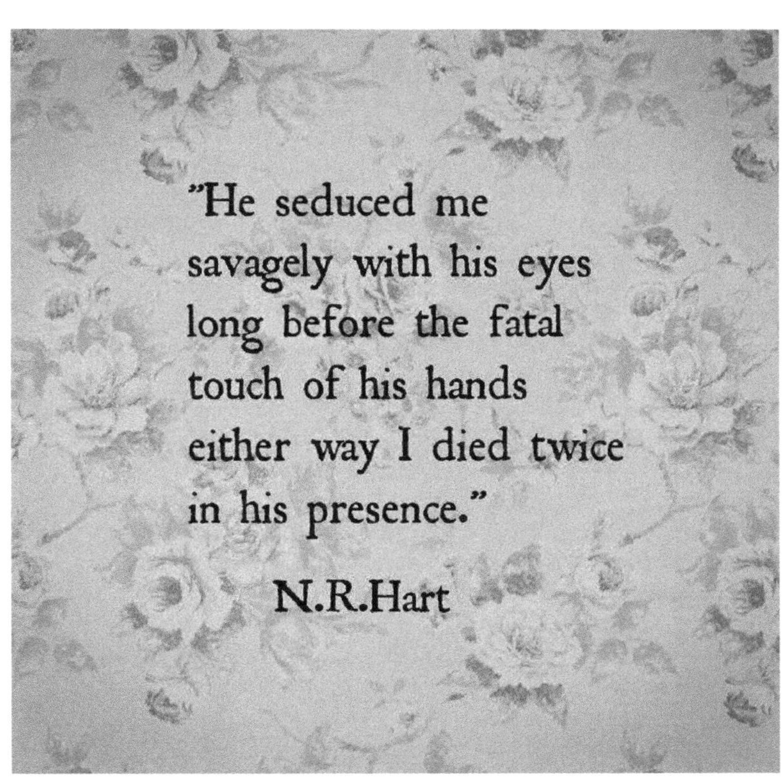
"He seduced me
savagely with his eyes
long before the fatal
touch of his hands
either way I died twice
in his presence."
N.R.Hart

"Twin Flames" part2

Twin flames known as souls split in two, when
the other half of your soul is bound to another
soul by familiarity and forged by fire. This pure
energy of the cosmos connects these souls on
every level.
Mentally, spiritually, soulfully and physically.
They are continually drawn and pulled towards one
another in mysterious ways through a powerful
force of the universe and return to each other again
and again like the crashing tides of the ocean.
Because this flame involves energy, the attraction
is so strong and fiery, it may even scare you off.
This connection feels so right to be together and
yet, there will be times you are separated from each
other and it will be painful. Everything feels wrong
in your life, like your entire world is empty without
them, and nothing makes sense until you are together
again. Their presence in your life shakes you up
and at the same time, you will feel at peace.
This "oneness" with another soul makes you feel
whole in ways you never have before. Like every
dying star has been brought back to life.
It feels like destiny to be with them. -N.R.Hart

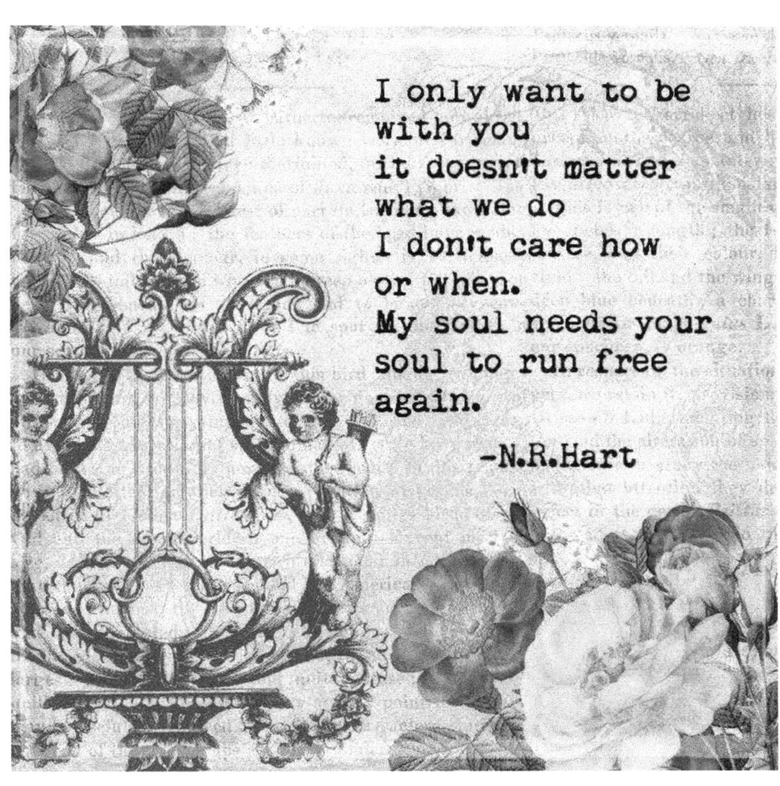
I only want to be
with you
it doesn't matter
what we do
I don't care how
or when.
My soul needs your
soul to run free
again.
-N.R.Hart

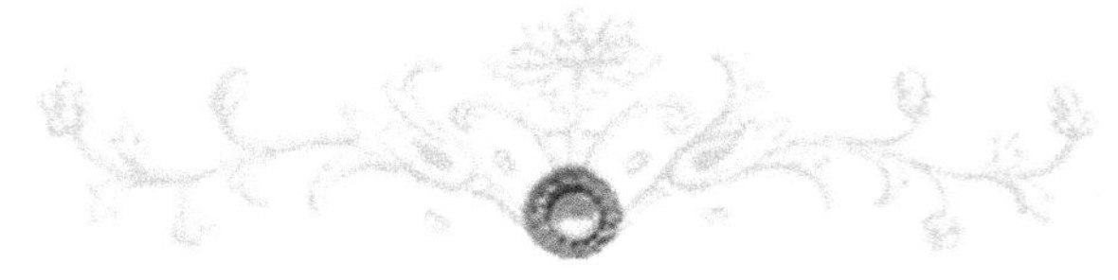

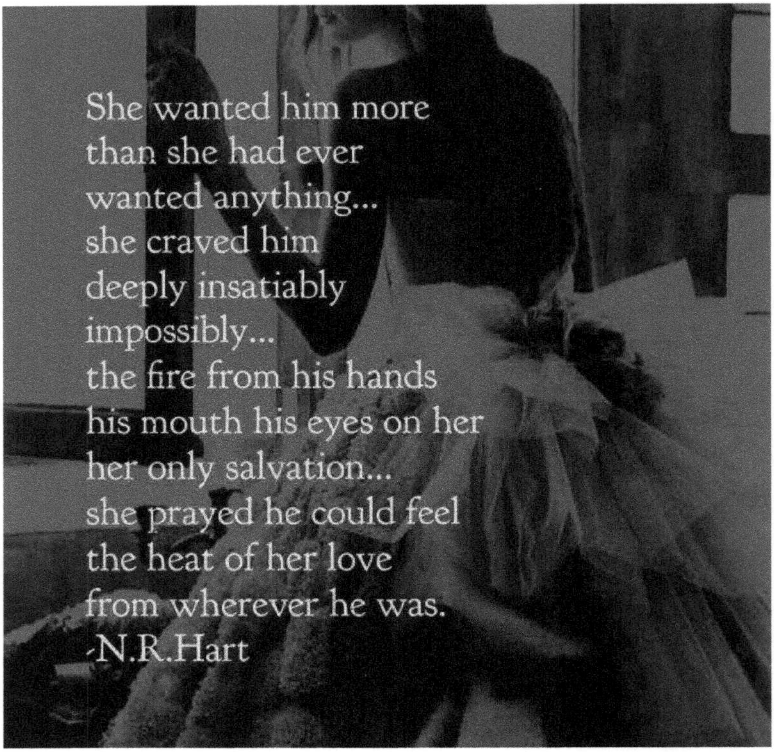

She wanted him more
than she had ever
wanted anything...
she craved him
deeply insatiably
impossibly...
the fire from his hands
his mouth his eyes on her
her only salvation...
she prayed he could feel
the heat of her love
from wherever he was.
-N.R.Hart

I liked it best when he took control
how he possessed me completely
the way I belonged to him
and he to me...
And this kind of power
makes you beautifully vulnerable
in ways that you show
your true self...
He was my safe place.
I loved him because
I could be me
in every way others never see.
-N.R.Hart "safe place"

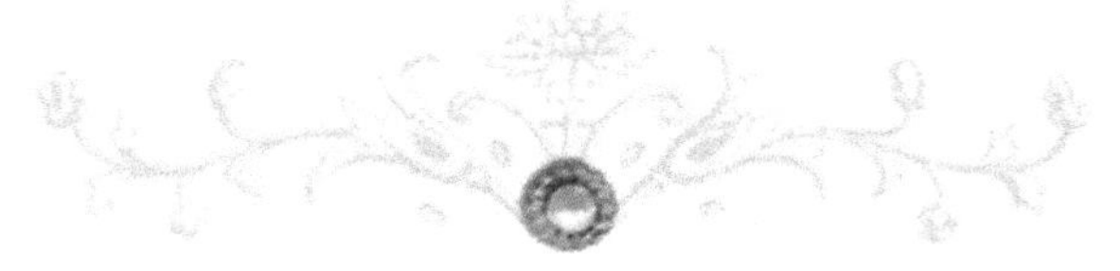

The most dangerous love
is the kind that starts a fire
in you that will not die and
every part of you is awakened...
from then on every other love
pales in comparison
never coming close to that alive
feeling you once had...
and what scares you the most is
what if you never love like that again?
As you feel yourself slowly dying
inside that cruelest realization.
-N.R.Hart

"Dangerous love"

I don't want to be the comfortable
one
I want to be the dangerous love.
The one you are mysteriously
drawn to
the one who keeps you up at night
makes your heart beat faster
an out of control love
that leaves you breathless.
I am not just any girl
I am your addiction.
The one you are wild for
the one you cannot live without.
I want to get under your skin and
stay there.

-N.R.Hart

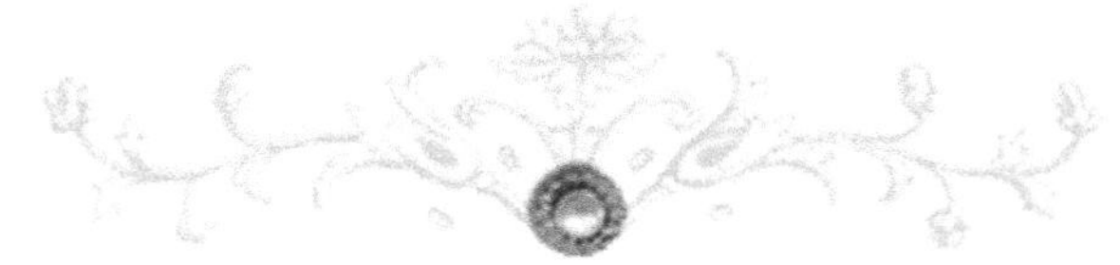

I would
rearrange
the stars
and align
the planets
hang the moon
and collide
like comets
cause madness
and mayhem
just to love you
again.

-N. R. Hart

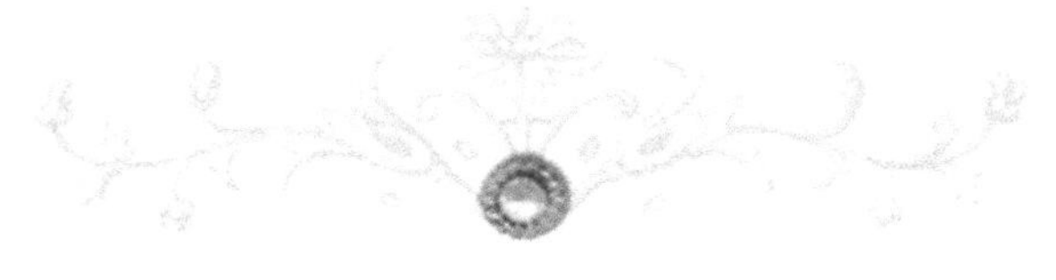

And tonight, it's just
you and me...
and there is nothing
I want more and nothing
else matters except
tonight...
and the sky is full of stars
and poems yet to be written
and sweet love to be made
kiss me now love me violent
love me well...
make me forget everything
everything but you.
-N.R.Hart

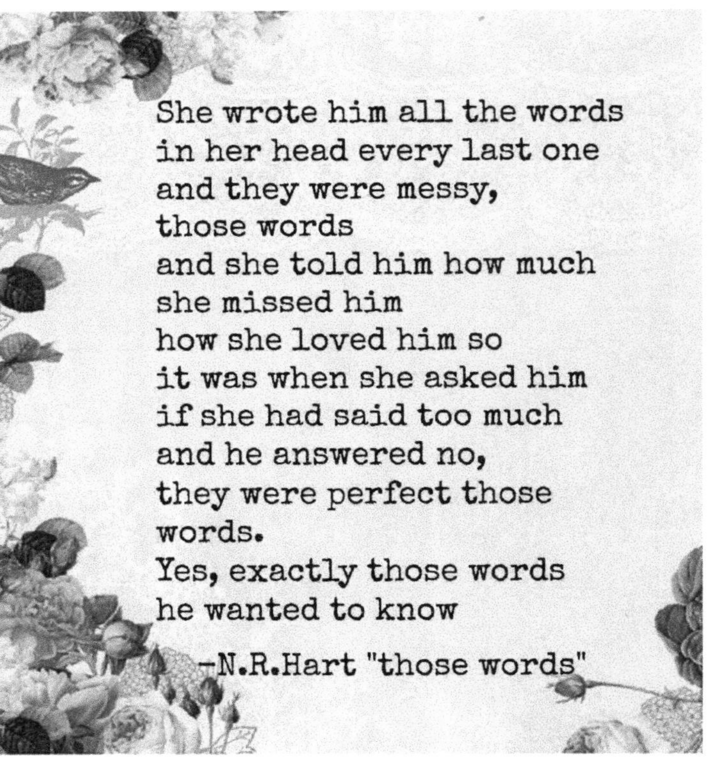
She wrote him all the words
in her head every last one
and they were messy,
those words
and she told him how much
she missed him
how she loved him so
it was when she asked him
if she had said too much
and he answered no,
they were perfect those
words.
Yes, exactly those words
he wanted to know
-N.R.Hart "those words"

It was peaceful as you drove
and I saw you sneaking
glances over at me
wondering if you knew
what I was thinking...
I stared out the window
and each moment was a
perfect stillness...
with my hand resting
inside yours
as the world blurred around us
and how I was falling
helplessly in love
with the world in you. -N.R.Hart

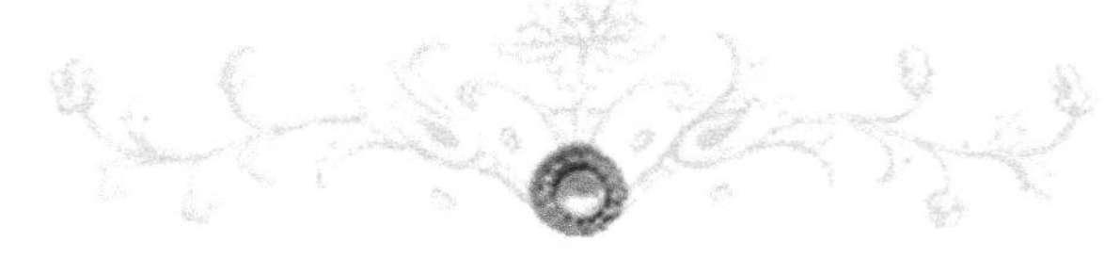

I remember the first time
your hand touched
my bare skin
a gasp escaped your lips
as your fingers traced
each soft curve
my burning flesh
now branded
with your imprint
you tasted like survival
on me
as I inhaled an addiction
to your touch.
-N.R.Hart

"The moment"

She was staring over at him
from the passenger seat, taking in his
presence. The air tasted of him
and he became everything...
her breathing, her pulse, her scenery
and she was having some trouble
concentrating.
Her heart was bursting with words
she longed to say, her mind racing
with so many thoughts...
she wanted to say things like "please
stay a little longer" or "I don't breathe
when you leave..."
her heart speaking the words perfectly
but never escaping her mouth.
Her soul split open screaming the words,
but it was too late, the moment was lost...
He was already gone. -N.R.Hart

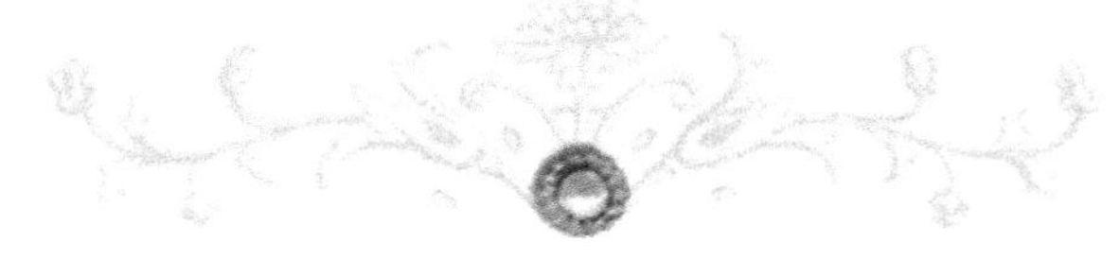

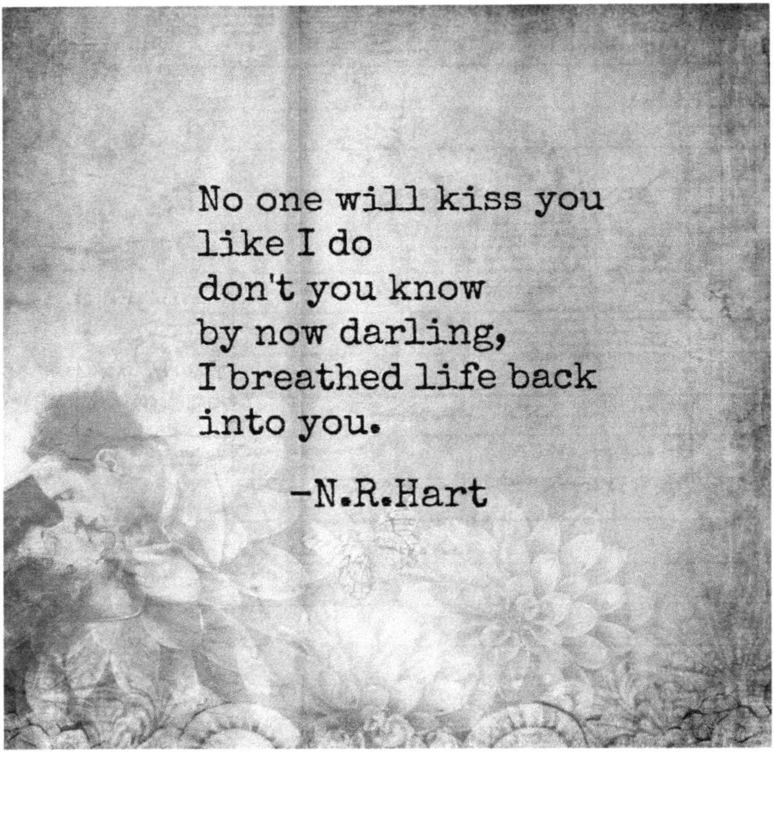

No one will kiss you
like I do
don't you know
by now darling,
I breathed life back
into you.

-N.R.Hart

I wasn't sure exactly when
I fell in love with you maybe
it was the wild beast in you
awakening the sleeping beauty
in me.
I got lost in your eyes
and never found
my way back again.
We were no fairytale
but rather a hot-blooded novel
an extraordinary love affair.
Our story may not have a happy
ending but oh, the loving
we did along the way...
You see, it was never
about the ending with us...
it was always about the story.

-N.R.Hart "no fairytale"

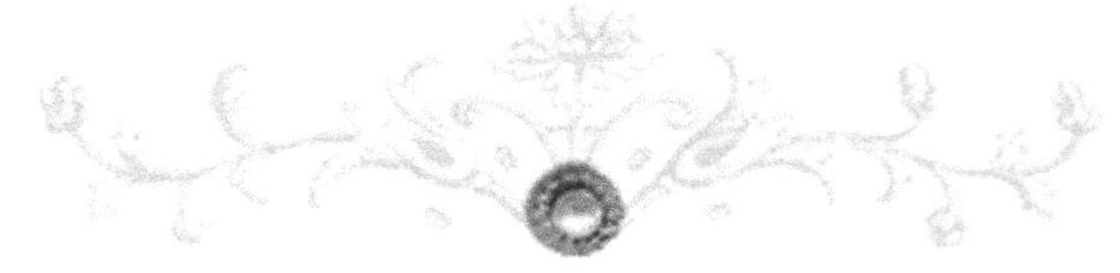

His hands grabbed
onto her hair
showing no mercy
as he took what he wanted
when he wanted
just the way she liked it
her body succumbed
to his every wish
as she felt herself losing
all control with him
it felt terrifying and right
as he possessed her body
claiming her soul.
He made her his.
It was a sweet dangerous
surrender. -N.R.Hart

Looking into her eyes he wasn't sure
what she was thinking. She always had
that faraway look as if she were
somewhere else and this made him wonder
what thoughts were running around in
her head and to his surprise...he
actually cared!
She made him feel things...all kinds
of things. Feelings he thought were
dead inside him for a very long time...
and for that he was grateful.
He felt alive again...but he also felt
vulnerable with her...like his soul
was exposed to her. It was something
he wasn't used to feeling....and it scared
him. She scared him...but all he knew
was...she made him feel loved again.

-N.R.Hart "love, his perspective"

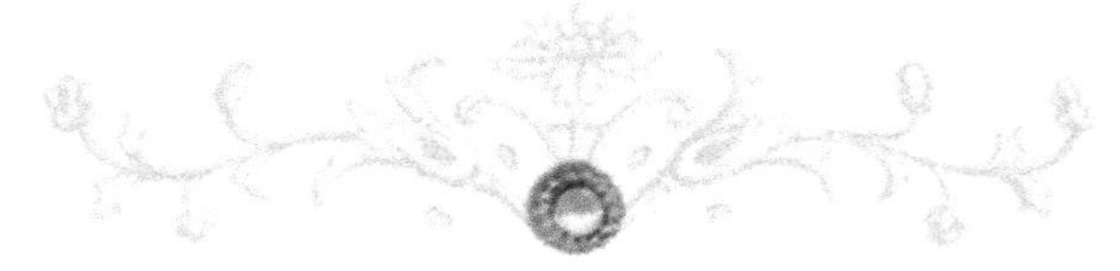

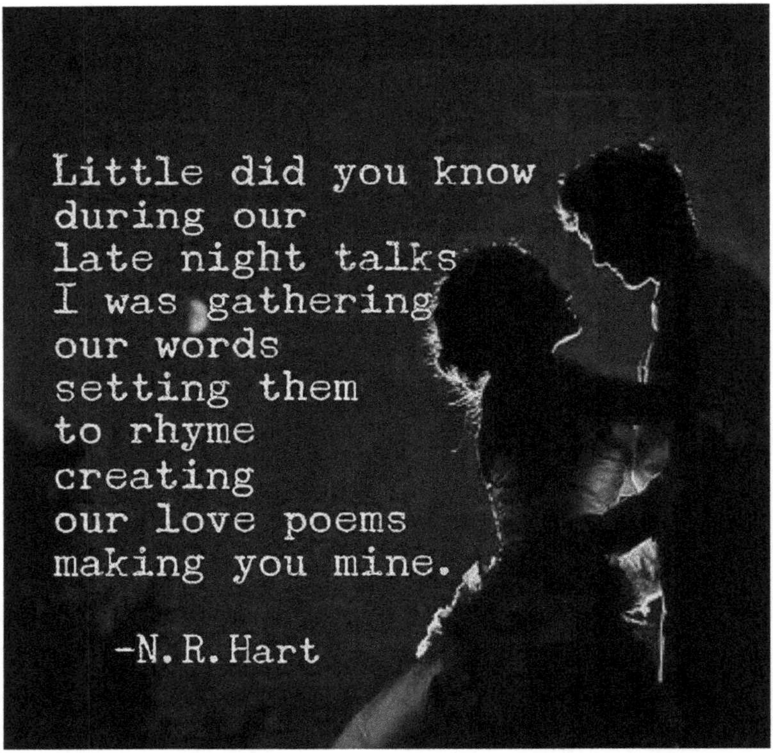

Little did you know
during our
late night talks
I was gathering
our words
setting them
to rhyme
creating
our love poems
making you mine.

-N.R.Hart

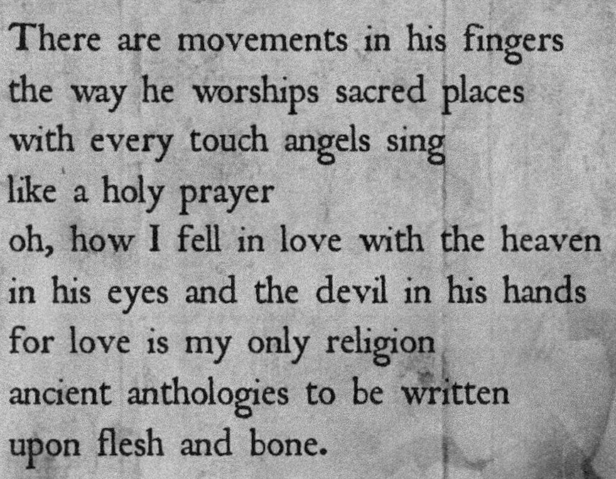
There are movements in his fingers
the way he worships sacred places
with every touch angels sing
like a holy prayer
oh, how I fell in love with the heaven
in his eyes and the devil in his hands
for love is my only religion
ancient anthologies to be written
upon flesh and bone.
-N.R.Hart "love is my only religion"

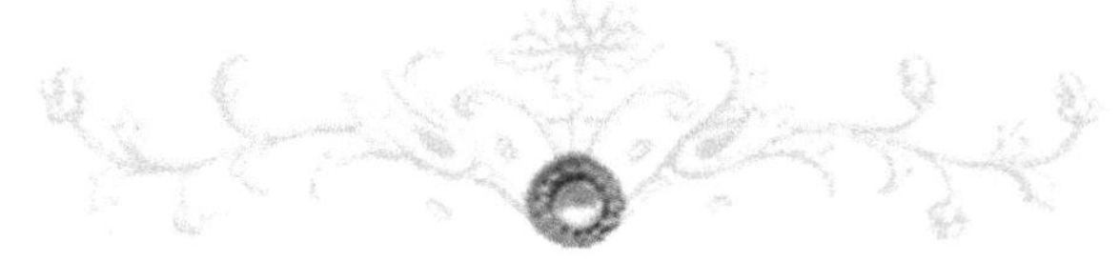

She looked at him
like he was
the only star
in her night sky
and she kissed him
like he was the air
keeping her alive.
-N.R.Hart

And it's bad tonight
this missing you...
I know you feel it too.
How can you not see
that looking into
each other's eyes...
is what we want
it's what we need.

-N.R.Hart

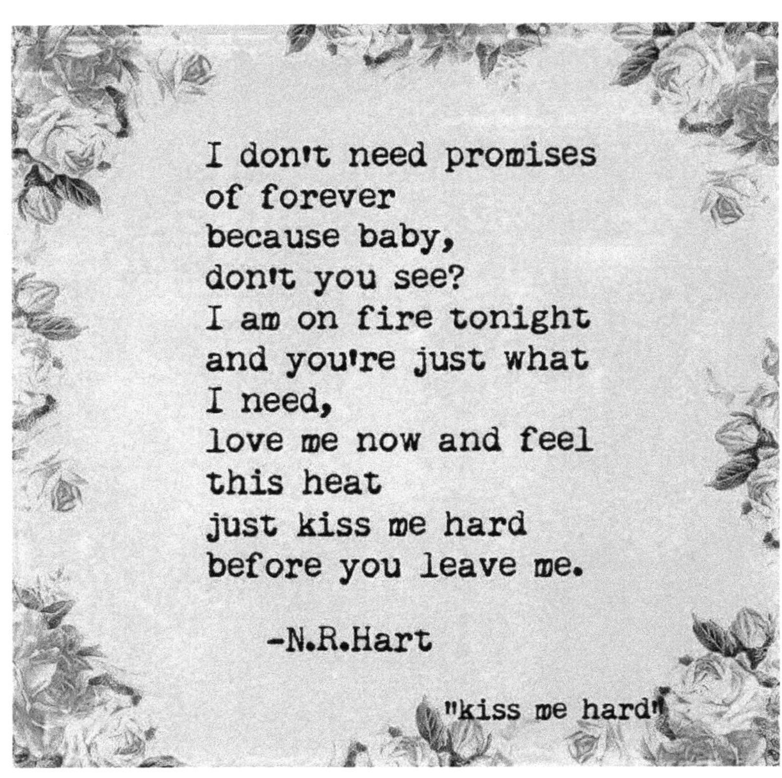
I don't need promises
of forever
because baby,
don't you see?
I am on fire tonight
and you're just what
I need,
love me now and feel
this heat
just kiss me hard
before you leave me.
-N.R.Hart
"kiss me hard"

Heaven and Hell

I am convinced there is one love
in your lifetime that you can never
forget and you will never get over.
It is different from all the rest
because it marks a before and after
them...in your life.
And it is the most terrifying kind
of love because you experience
a passion that is out of control...
it excites you and scares you
at the same time. You become addicted
to that feeling of being alive.
And this kind of love...and only
this kind you would move heaven
and earth...meet them on the other
side of hell...just to feel it again.

N.R.Hart

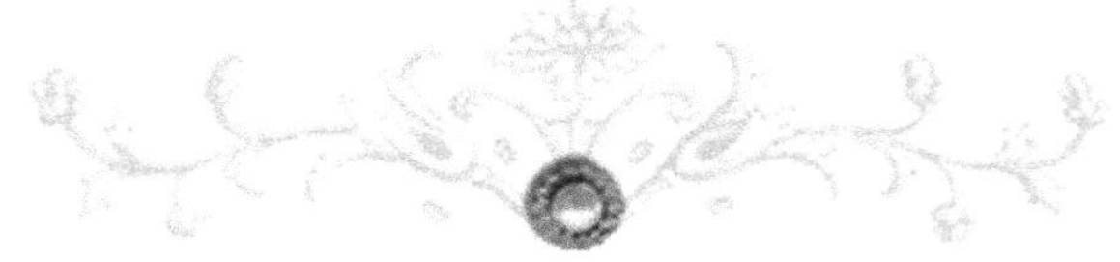

More - Part2

I want to kiss you like sweet lingering kisses.
Something like the moon and stars
or like something I keep trying hard to reach.
How do I show you how I feel. Can kisses do that.
Maybe if I kiss you deep enough I can somehow
touch your soul with my breath.
And, I cannot wait any longer to see you,
to crawl onto your lap looking into your eyes,
wrapping my hands around your neck,
pulling you close, kissing you long and deep.
This was one kiss of so much more to come.
My hands found their way to your shoulders and
down even further. I needed to reach for that
pulsing heat in you. Can you feel the hunger in
my kiss. I am not certain of many things in this
life but I know that my mouth is starving for
yours. And, I know that I am in love with how your
body fits with mine. If we are not made for each
other, then tell me, please god tell me, why do our
bodies already know this to be true? You see,
this is a desperate love, a persistent love,
an urgent love. And, I need you now... -N.R.Hart

Chasing starlight

I looked deep into
your eyes that night
chasing starlight
as you were staring
into mine...
a beautiful collision
of darkness and light
the sun and moon
crashing as one...
hand in hand together
we run.

-N.R.Hart

I remember sitting there with you
in the burning sunlight
staring into your eyes and wanting
nothing more than to escape there
softly melting into one another
as the rest of the world faded away...
and it was just the two of us sweetly
soaking in each other's presence.
You tenderly put your arm around me
as my hair spilled into your hands
and we just sat there for the longest
time saying nothing.
And, I wondered how it was...
I could feel so peaceful with you
and at the same time, *on fire*.

-N.R.Hart "on fire"

All the stars
in the night sky
and I was never
so starstruck
by the ones
in your eyes.
-N.R.Hart

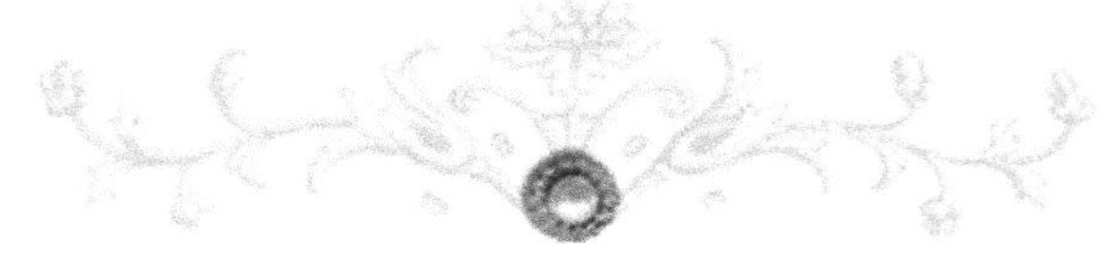

I really thought I
was strong enough
to stand on my
own two feet but
your touch...it
brings me
to my knees.
-N.R.Hart

Love her tenderly
so she feels
the love in your heart
love her savagely
so she burns from
the fire in your soul.

-N. R. Hart

I am scared I will forget
the sound of your voice.
The way you feel...
how your eyes rest on me.
The thrill of you...
the way your hands set me
on fire.
I breathe differently
with you...
I feel more like me.
I don't ever want to forget
how I am...
when I'm with you.

And, I am scared. -N.R.Hart

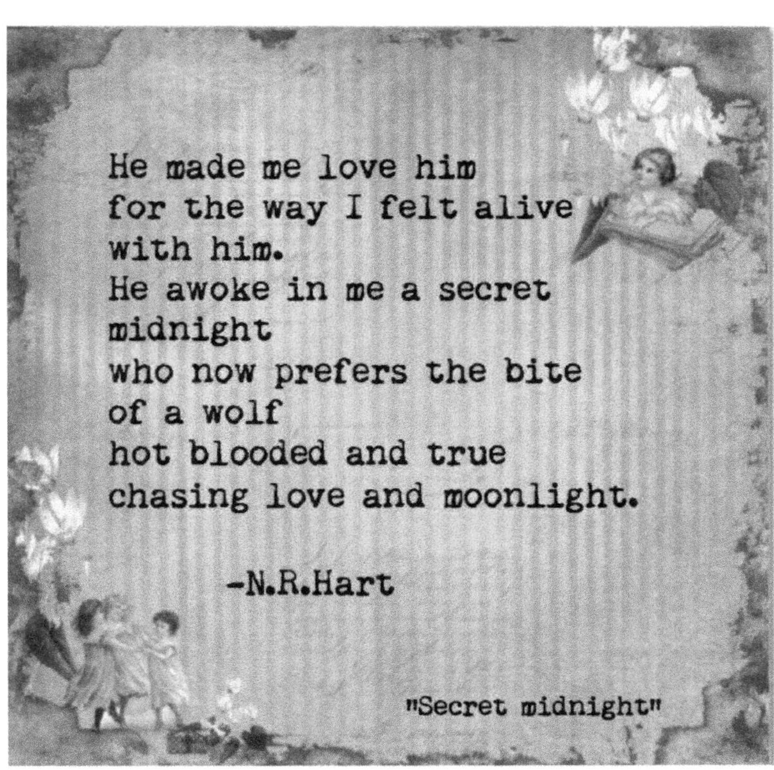
He made me love him
for the way I felt alive
with him.
He awoke in me a secret
midnight
who now prefers the bite
of a wolf
hot blooded and true
chasing love and moonlight.
-N.R.Hart
"Secret midnight"

I tried to remember the last time
I looked into your eyes
because staring into them tonight
I felt everything come back to me.
How familiar we are
how safe we feel together
how long we have craved each other
ached for each other
how we don't even need words
because they just get in the way.
And, how staring back into your eyes
I felt so many things I have never felt
with anyone but you
but mostly, how I belonged to you.
Your eyes told me everything
you could not say, but I already knew.
I have always known.
I've been yours all along. -N.R.Hart

HOW WAS I
TO KNOW THIS
TINY SPARK
WOULD SPREAD
LIKE
WILDFIRES.
-N.R. HART

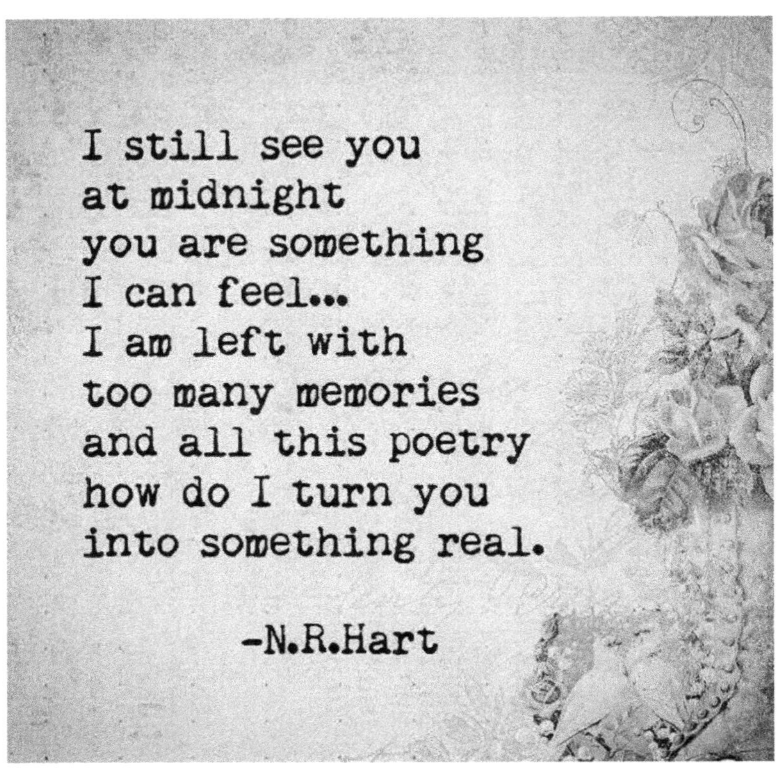
I still see you
at midnight
you are something
I can feel...
I am left with
too many memories
and all this poetry
how do I turn you
into something real.
-N.R.Hart

"A midsummer night's dream"
My summer love
where have you
gone?
Awaiting for you
to come upon me
But it was only a
midsummer night's
dream
As I awoke to the sound
of the September rain
washing you away.
-N.R.Hart

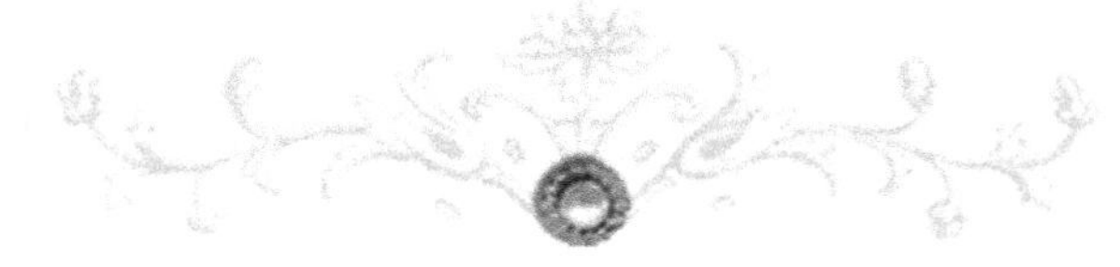

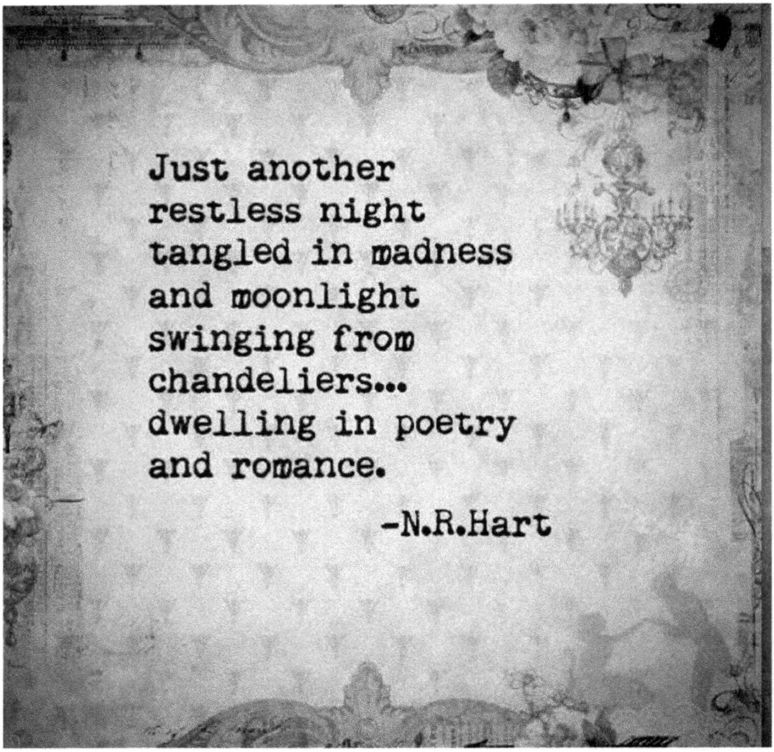

Just another
restless night
tangled in madness
and moonlight
swinging from
chandeliers...
dwelling in poetry
and romance.

-N.R.Hart

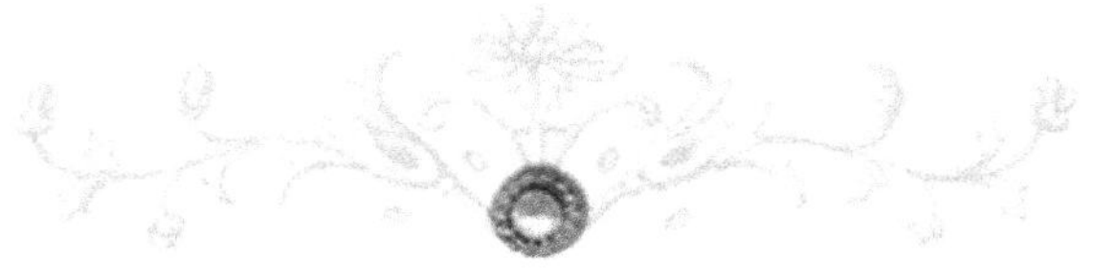

An Autumn Season

"Souls tend to go back to who

feels like home."

N.R.Hart

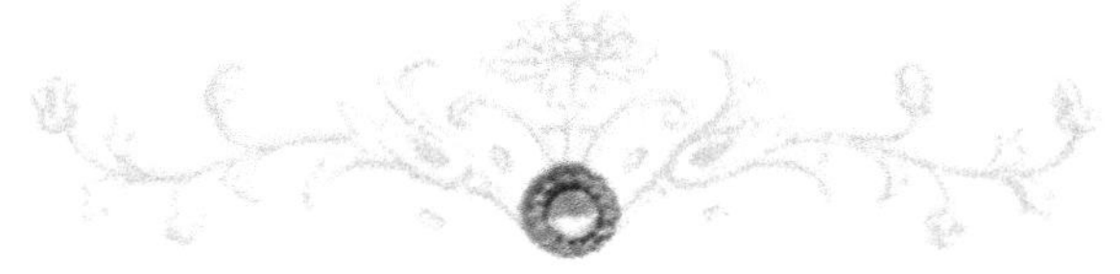

A Heart Story

He held her heart
in his hands and she
wasn't entirely certain
if he would drop it
break it or just keep it
safe with him
but for now she just loved
the feel of his hands there.

- N.R. Hart

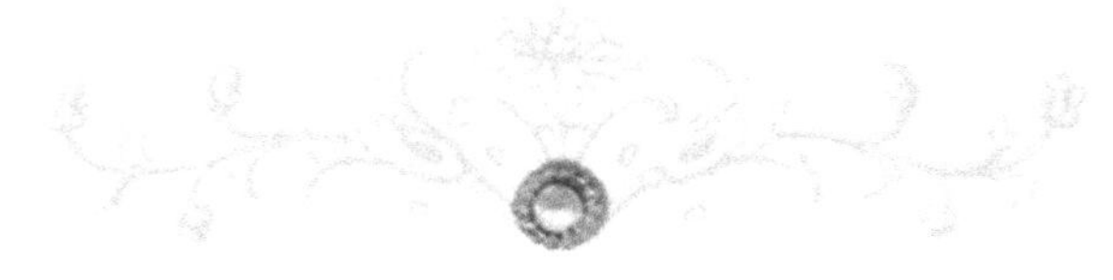

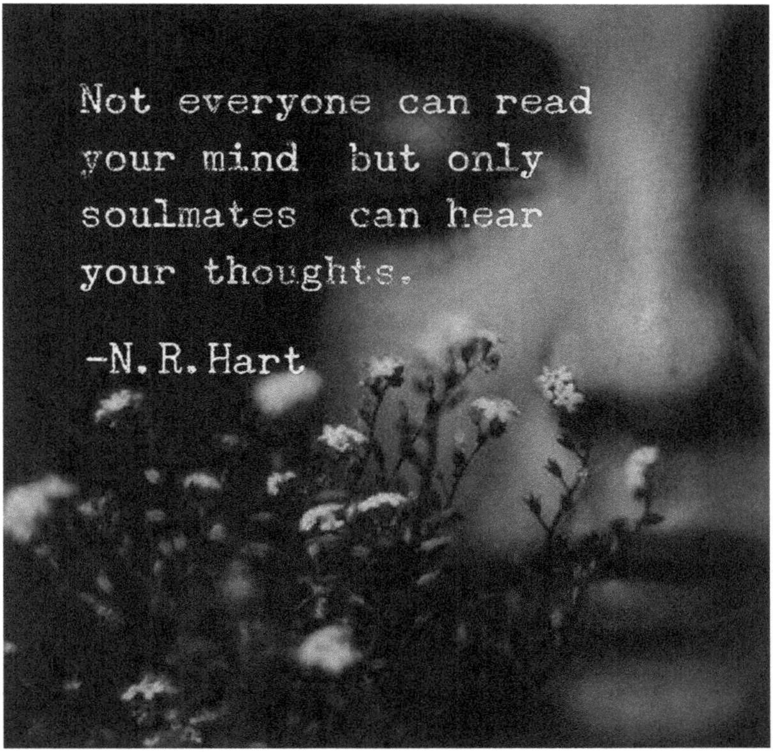

Not everyone can read
your mind but only
soulmates can hear
your thoughts.

-N.R.Hart

Moon child

Your eyes so full of grace
and fire
how fragile you appear
my little moon child
crystal tears full of wonderment
and fear
we are the same your shadow
and mine
staying up late to question
the moon
you never needed the answers
to your questions
carrying the entire universe
in your eyes
you just go on shining....
lighting up the entire sky.

-N.R.Hart

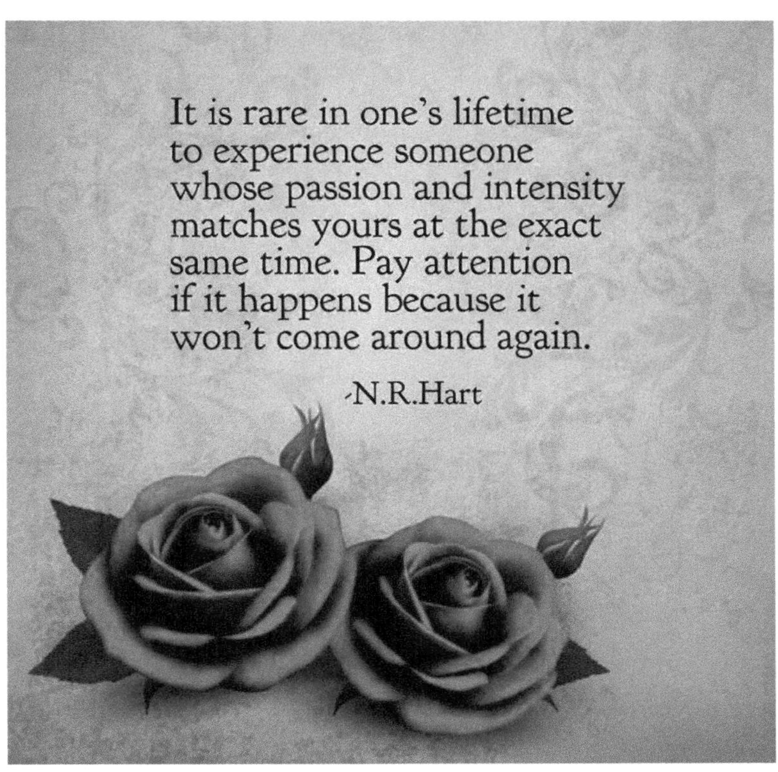
It is rare in one's lifetime
to experience someone
whose passion and intensity
matches yours at the exact
same time. Pay attention
if it happens because it
won't come around again.
-N.R.Hart

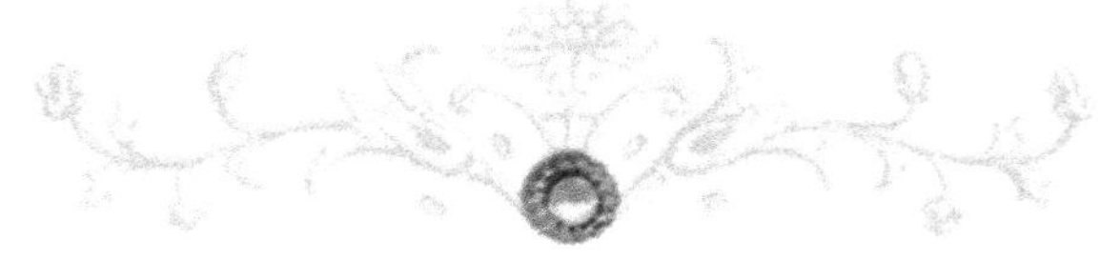

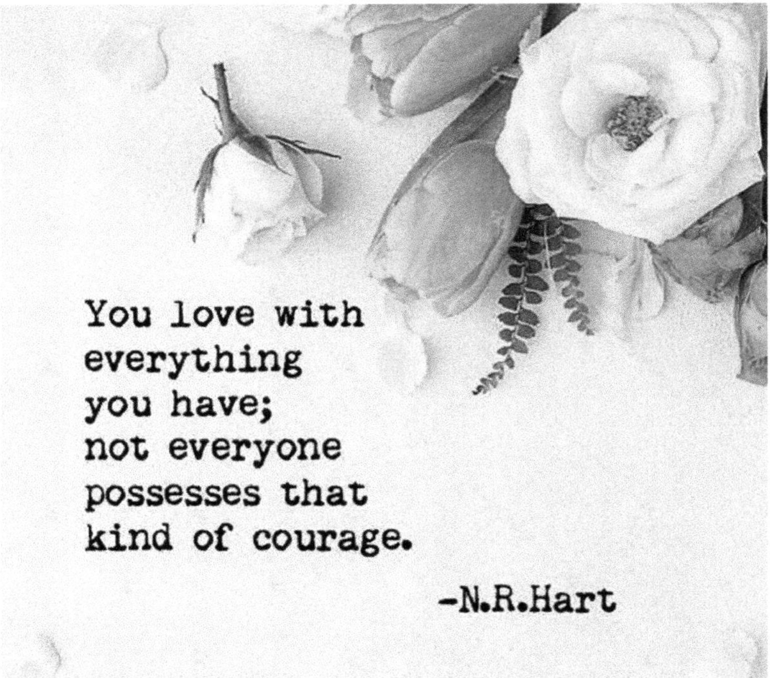

You love with
everything
you have;
not everyone
possesses that
kind of courage.

-N.R.Hart

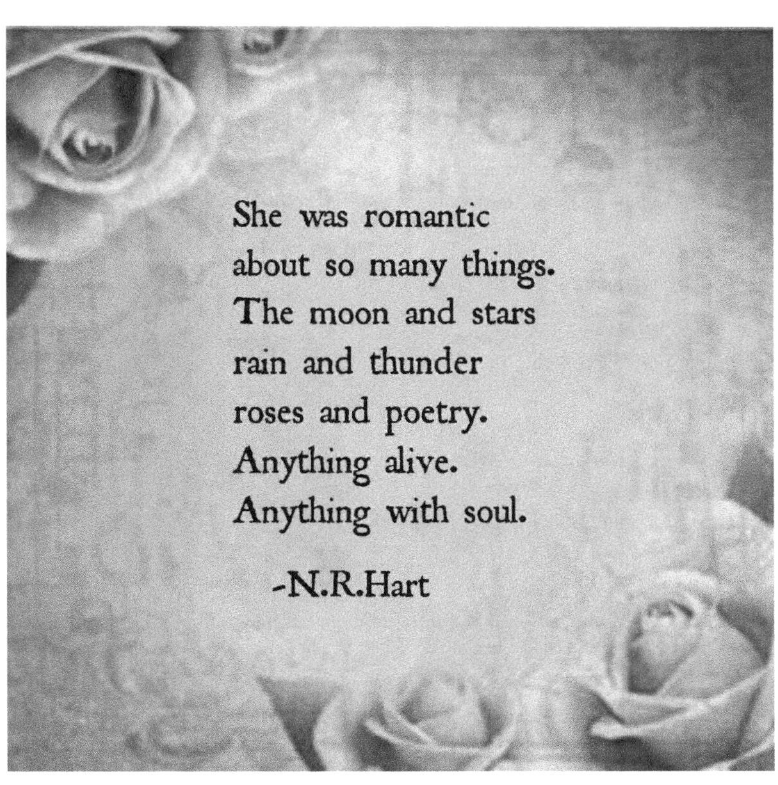
She was romantic
about so many things.
The moon and stars
rain and thunder
roses and poetry.
Anything alive.
Anything with soul.
-N.R.Hart

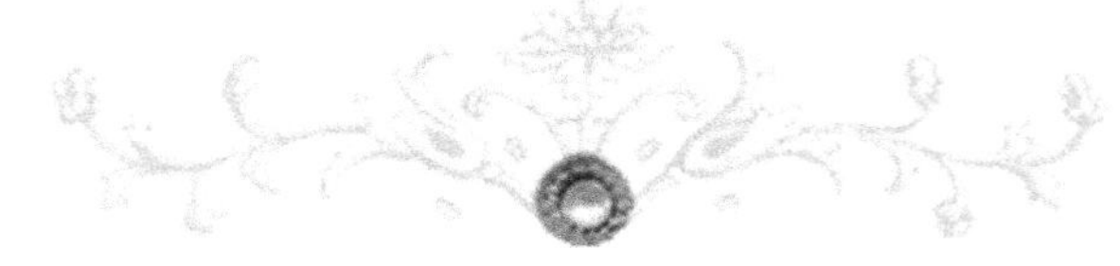

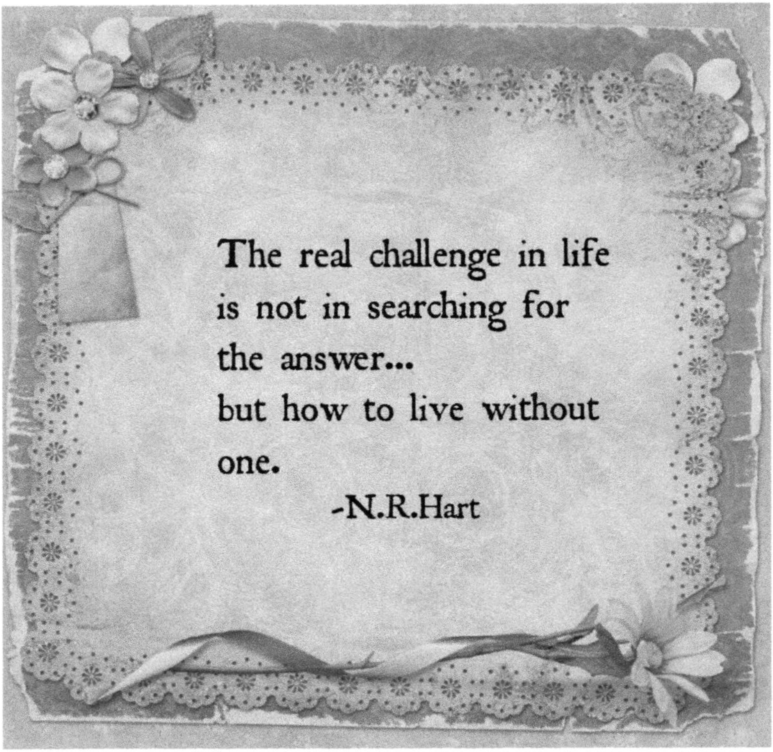

The real challenge in life
is not in searching for
the answer...
but how to live without
one.
-N.R.Hart

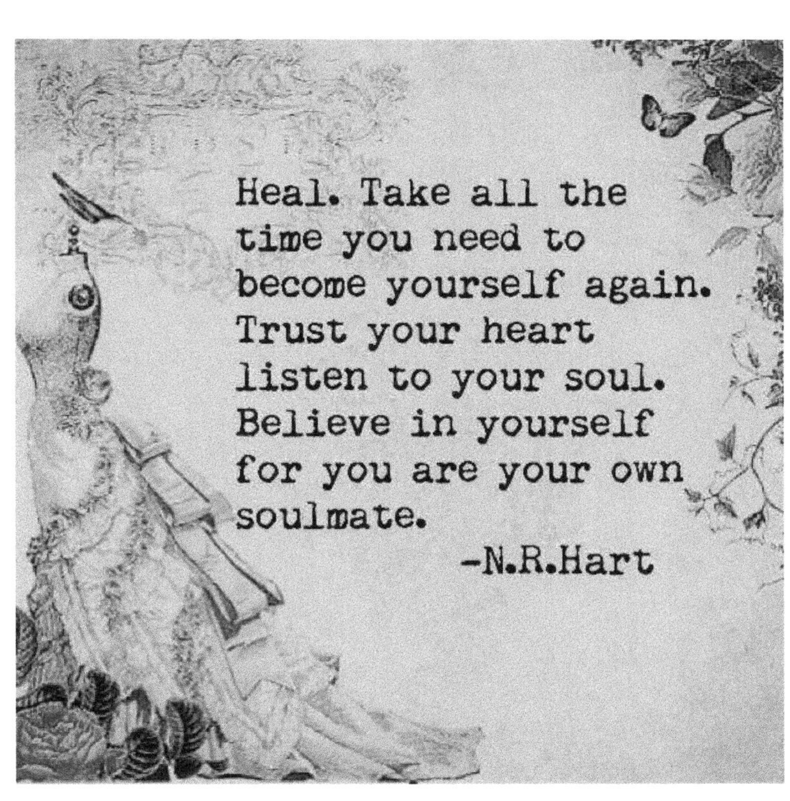
Heal. Take all the
time you need to
become yourself again.
Trust your heart
listen to your soul.
Believe in yourself
for you are your own
soulmate.
-N.R.Hart

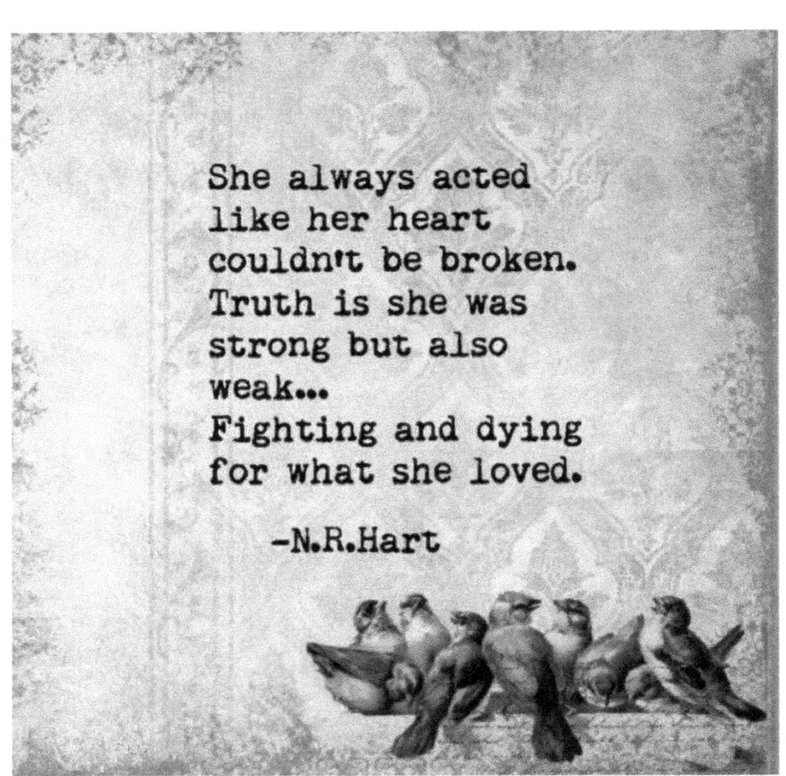
She always acted
like her heart
couldn't be broken.
Truth is she was
strong but also
weak...
Fighting and dying
for what she loved.
-N.R.Hart

"Look a little closer
in those delicate eyes
her heart's a wild creature
and her soul's on fire."
-N.R.Hart

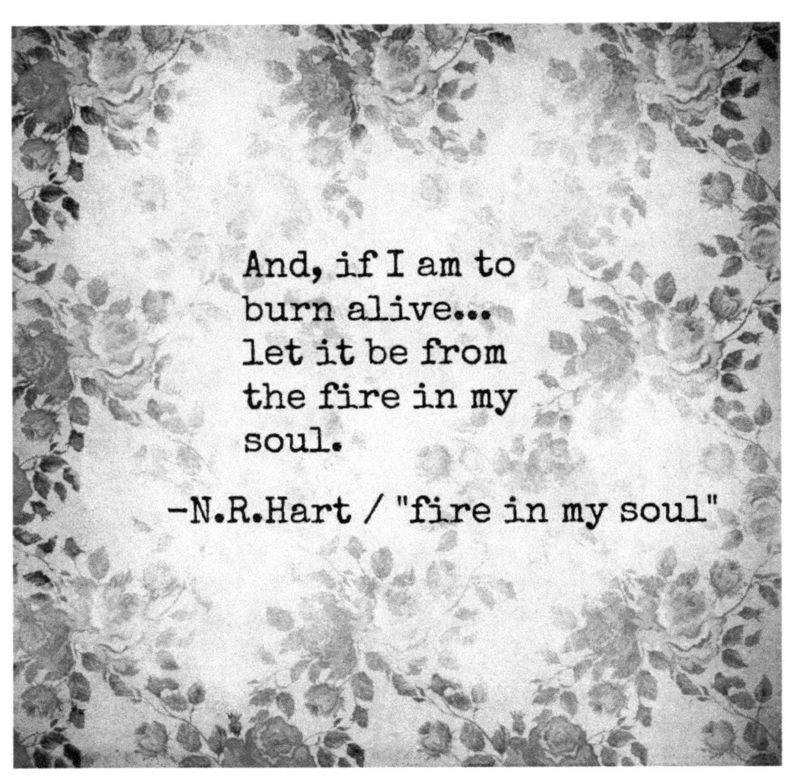
And, if I am to
burn alive...
let it be from
the fire in my
soul.
-N.R.Hart / "fire in my soul"

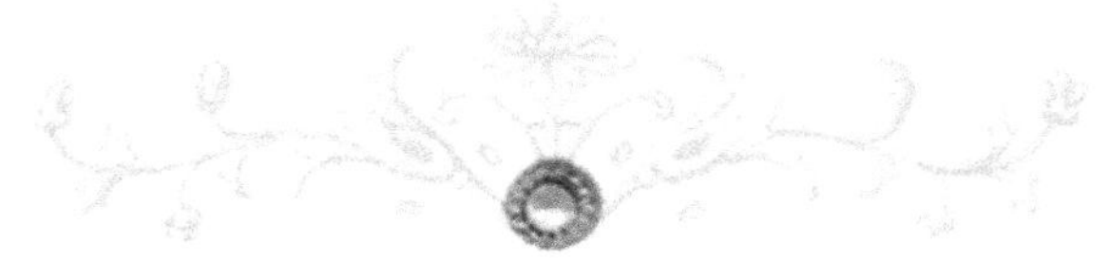

There will always be words
that penetrate your mind
memories stabbing your heart
a kiss that is still
burning your lips
and a love that pierces your
soul forever. -N.R.Hart

I don't want safe.
I want danger. I want passion.
I don't want ordinary
breathing.
I want to catch my breath
each time I think
of you.
I want extraordinary
like the heat in your touch.
I am tired of the cold.
Even if I have to write it
I will live it.
I want to burn inside
these pages of poetry.

-N.R.Hart "pages of poetry"

You said goodbye
to her didn't you?
And you were
thinking
she was just
one star
there are
millions more
until it hits you
she wasn't
just any star
she lit up
your whole
damn universe.
-N.R.Hart

You can deny your
feelings all you want
pretend you don't
feel anything...
but your heart knows
who you can't stop
thinking about...
You can never fool
your own heart.
I would rather
suffer for you...
suffer for passion
than not feel anything
at all.-N.R.Hart

There are some people you meet
and you know somehow,
they are not like anyone else.
They will have an important place
in your life.
These people will mean something
different to you because you feel
them deep in your soul.
You come alive with them near.
They represent many things to you.
Love, freedom, happiness...
It is not possible to forget them
They will last the longest
on your mind. -N.R.Hart
"unforgettable"

"Stories"

Maybe we are all just stories...
stories of love
stories of hope, of despair.
Stories of how we are looking for love,
how we found love, what we did for
love...what we didn't do.
To all those scared and running from
love...stay and make a story.
Love is a precious gift. It's a rare thing.
Accept it graciously.
Don't run from your story.
It will be all you have left
one day.... -N.R.Hart

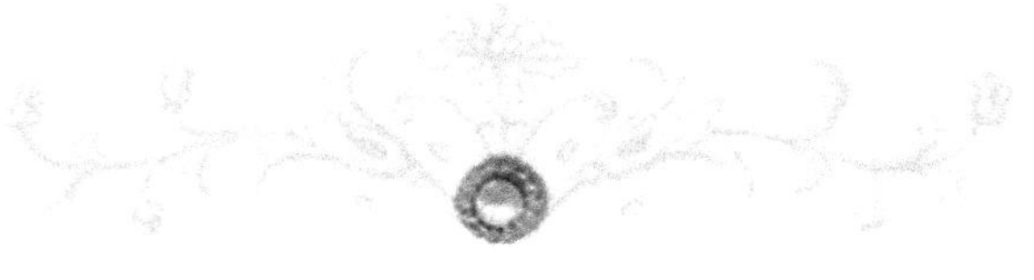

I warned you
I am not like those
other girls who are
scared of love...
I do not fear loving
you.
If you want to continue
to be half-loved
then let them...
I have no limits
when it comes to love
I will hand over my soul
to you
I am not afraid...

N.R. Hart

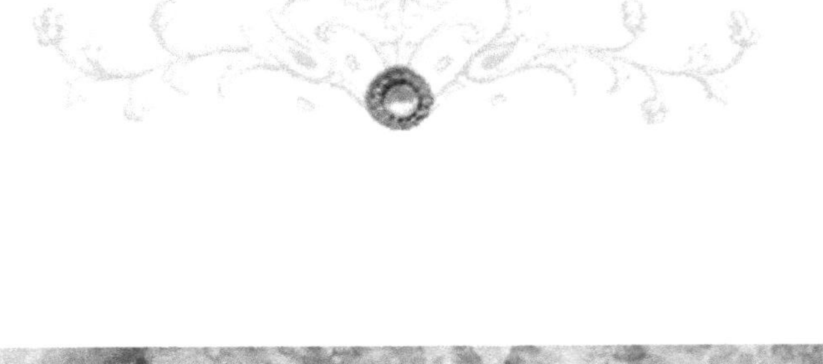

Maybe you weren't mine
but it felt like we
belonged to each other
and I loved you as though
you were mine.
-N.R.Hart

She's a hopeless romantic
but not the kind you think of...
she's beauty and chaos tangled
in confusion and love...
she'll risk shattering heartbreak
as her true desires unfold...
she's devastatingly romantic
despairingly vulnerable
down to her soul...
she aches for love and passion
to arrive ...
and just needs someone to move her
so she knows she's alive.

– N.R. Hart

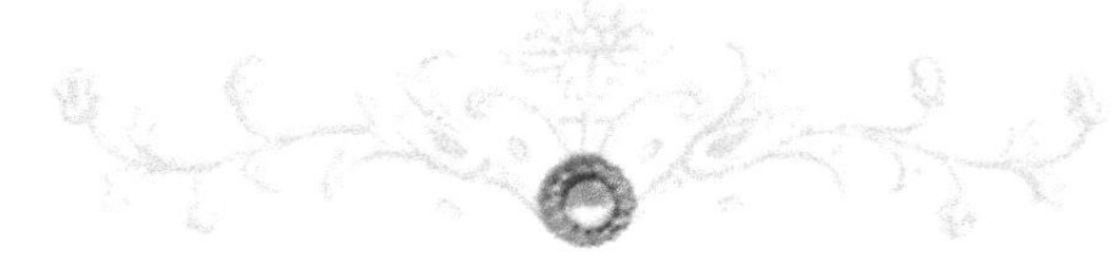

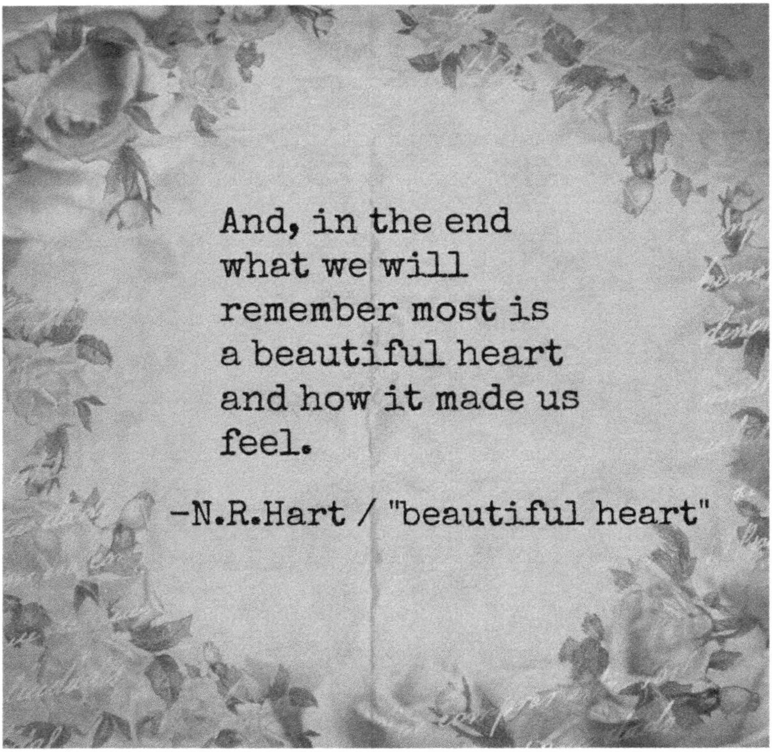

And, in the end
what we will
remember most is
a beautiful heart
and how it made us
feel.

-N.R.Hart / "beautiful heart"

Pearls of wisdom
"she turned her
pain into poetry
her darknesss
into beauty
and her scars into
pearls of wisdom."
-N.R.Hart

I find beauty in things others never see.
I find hope there too. Life is what you make
it. Life is taking not so beautiful things
and making them beautiful. It is finding
hope even when there is none.
This is not an easy thing to do but
I find that love is the answer to most
things, if not all things. Why not love
more? If you do not give your love away,
then it means nothing. In essence, it is a
wasted love. No one will ever feel it. Love
is meant to be felt. To be given away freely,
regardless of what you get back in return.
We all want our lives to have meaning. So we
can say we were here and we loved with
everything we had. My life is not perfect
but it's mine and I never wanted perfect. I
want real. I want to feel. And, I have loved,
really loved. A lot. And, above all I have
lived really lived. And god, I still love.

-N.R.Hart "Life"

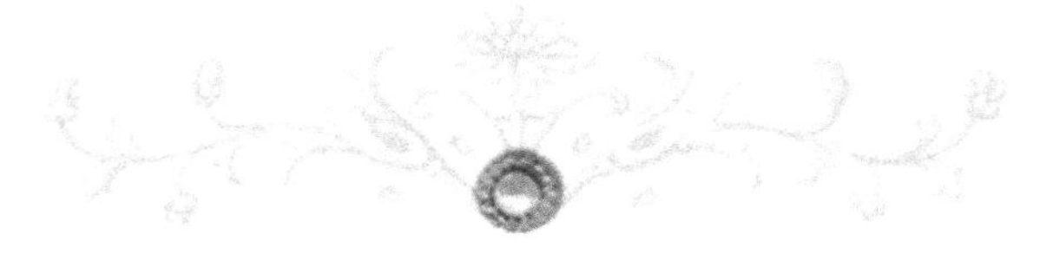

"Love story"

"Are you just going to leave me here
to write my own ending?

We lived this love story and
these words...
they wrote themselves.
But, I won't write the ending...
not just yet. Because, there is still
so much more to feel. Just put your hand
in mine and never let go."

-N.R.Hart

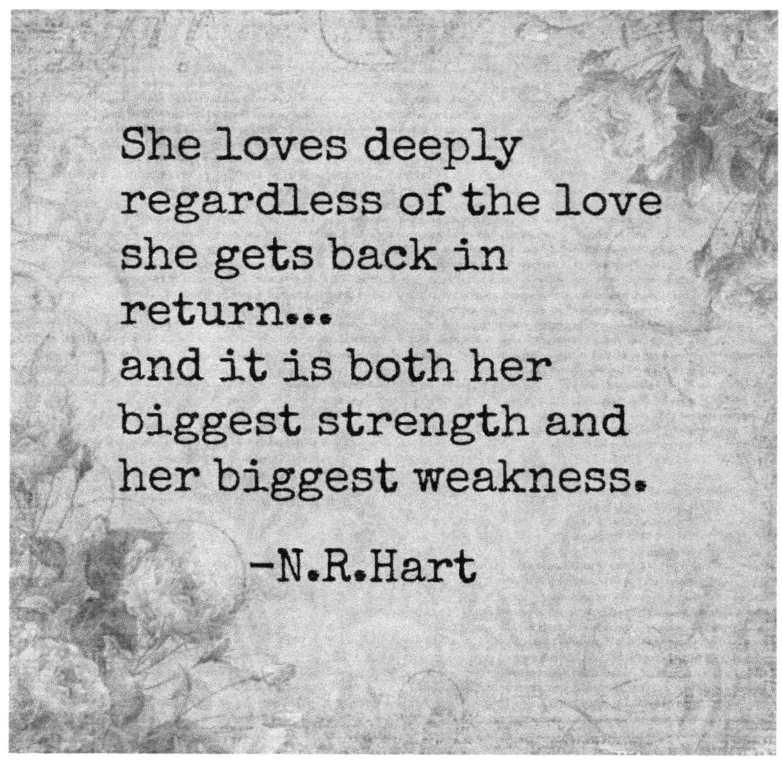
She loves deeply
regardless of the love
she gets back in
return...
and it is both her
biggest strength and
her biggest weakness.
-N.R.Hart

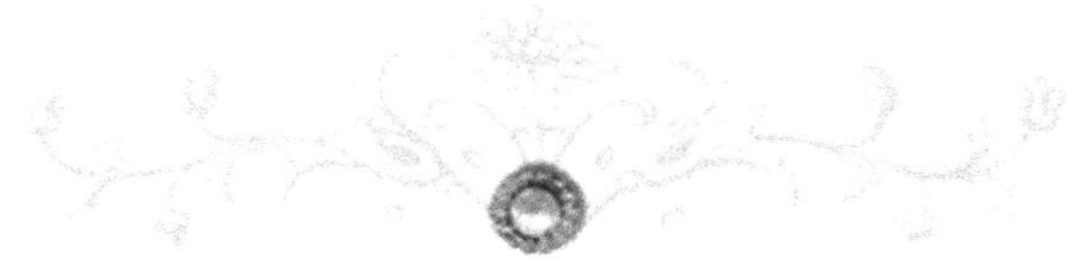

I was different with you
I felt more like myself.
And oftentimes I return
to our favorite spot
to lose myself
in your memory
just to find myself
again.

- N.R. Hart

She is haunted by her
own heart
and the love she hides
inside.
-N.R.Hart "haunted heart"

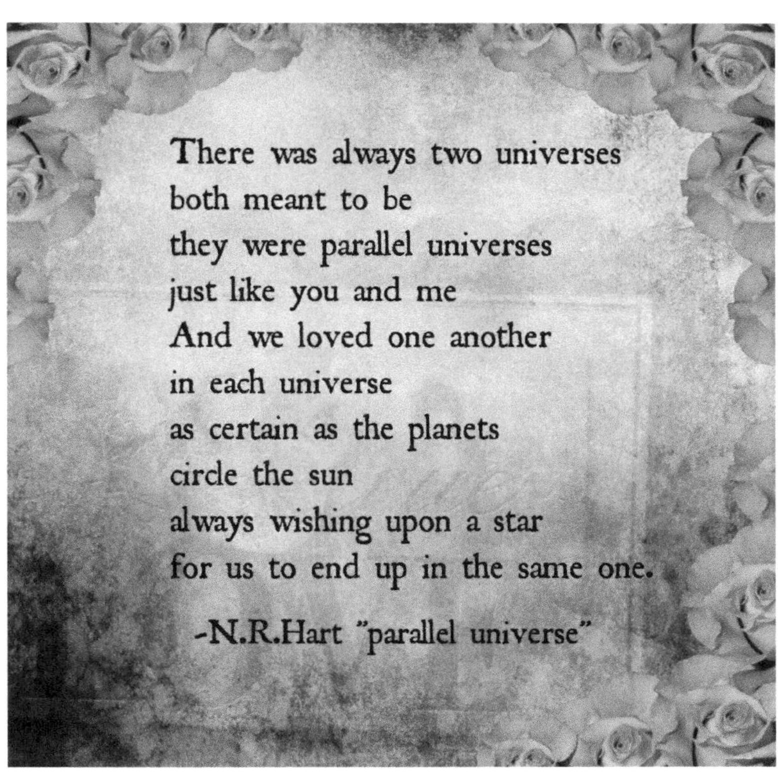
There was always two universes
both meant to be
they were parallel universes
just like you and me
And we loved one another
in each universe
as certain as the planets
circle the sun
always wishing upon a star
for us to end up in the same one.
-N.R.Hart "parallel universe"

If you are alone
and I will sit there with you
if you are weak
and I will give you my blood
my bones
if you are scared
and I will hold you close
and closer still
if you can no longer live
and I will love you
back to life.
I feel so much of you
inside me
and I am no longer certain
where you begin and I end.
-N.R.Hart "beginning and end"

SOMETIMES THE
BRAVEST THING
YOU CAN DO IS LET
SOMEONE LOVE YOU.
-N.R.HART

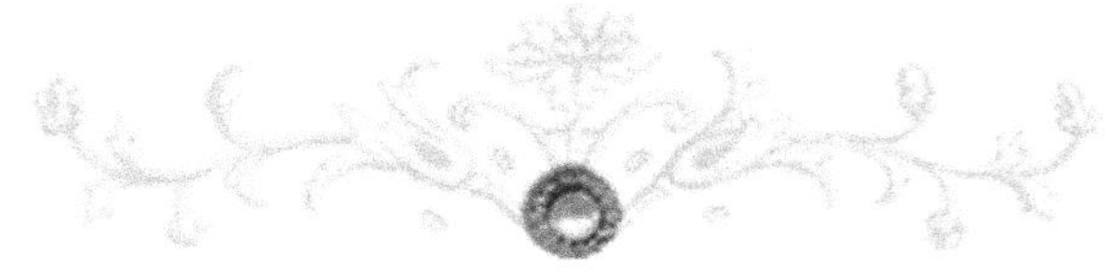

Their chemistry was volatile from
the start..friends, lovers, soulmates
they were all of it together.
They were connected by a fiery energy
on a deep soulful level with an intense
magnetic attraction to one another.
Not only were their minds in sync
reading one another's thoughts, so
were their bodies.
He knew her body like the back of his
hand. He knew when she needed a soft
caress or a firm grip. How she craved
the fine line between pleasure and
pain. He knew what she needed even
before she knew herself. He knew how to
give her what she was afraid to ask for.
And, just like twin flames that will not
die, it lives inside you burning
you alive. -N.R.Hart *(twin flames)*

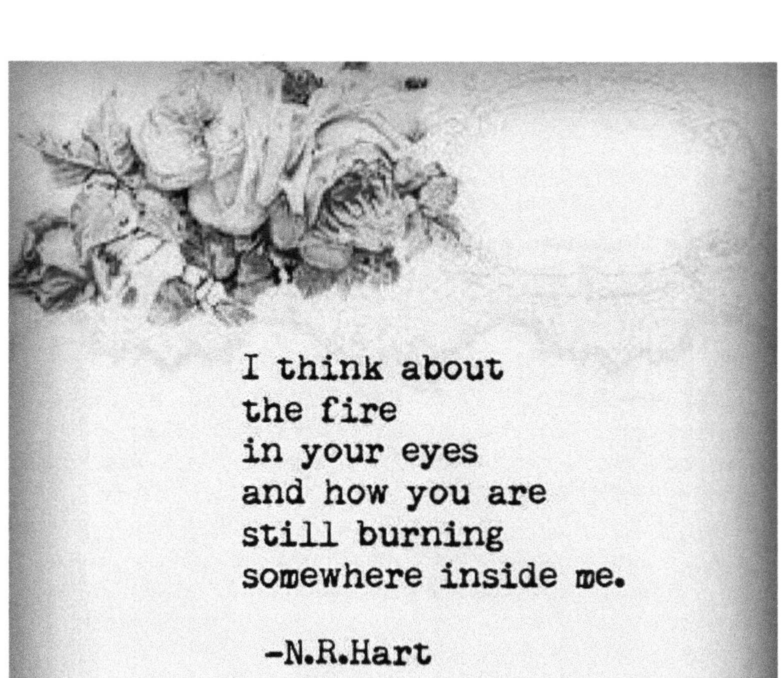
I think about
the fire
in your eyes
and how you are
still burning
somewhere inside me.
-N.R.Hart

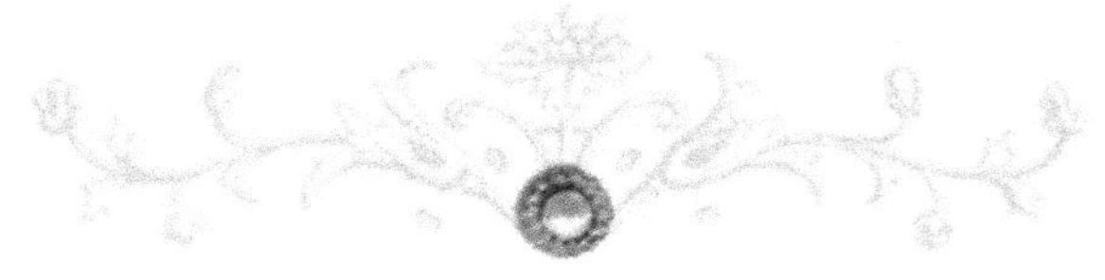

She's the girl you never saw coming,
the unexpected one who calms you, centers you, and
still she turns out to be the surprise
love of your life.
She gets you, really gets you like no one ever has.
She is your best friend, lover and soulmate all
wrapped up in the prettiest package.
She is unforgettable, she is like no one, which is
why you are addicted to her, her mind, her soul.
You can't get her out of your system. You taste her
and she runs through you hot like blood and fire.
She never leaves you no matter what, because
she too, knows how rare the connection is. You have
never had anyone stick by you like that before.
She is the safest place you have ever known.
You are soft for her no matter how hard life gets,
she is there and your feelings never change. She
loves you fiercely and you feel her love deep in
your bones, in your soul.
She is the one who makes you feel whole in a way
you never have before and that terrifies you.
But what terrifies you even more...is losing her.

-N.R.Hart "unexpected"

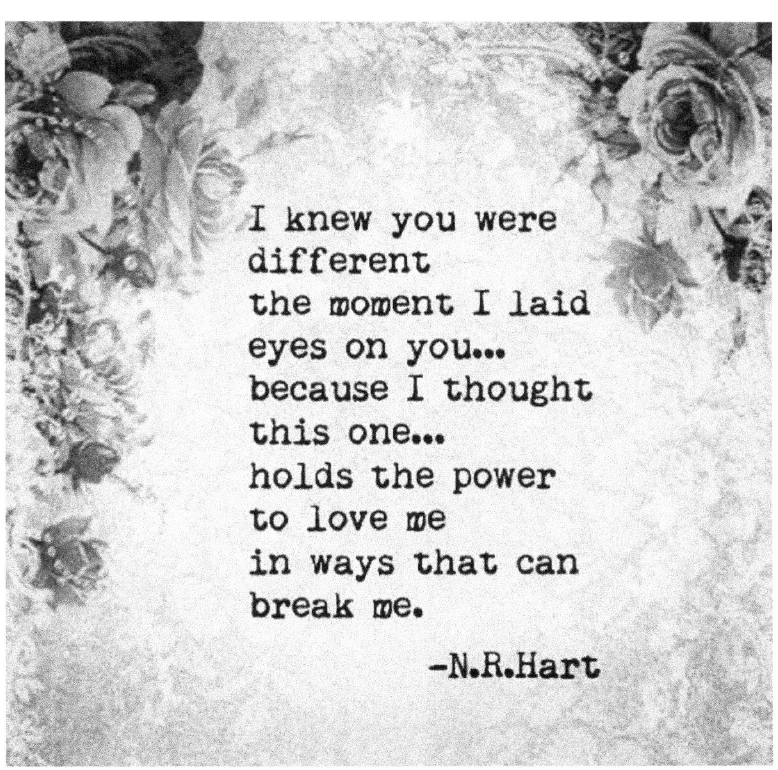
I knew you were
different
the moment I laid
eyes on you...
because I thought
this one...
holds the power
to love me
in ways that can
break me.
-N.R.Hart

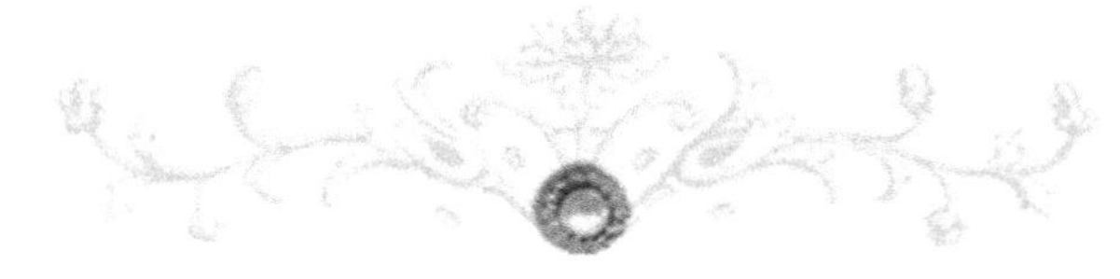

"My soul is in love with your soul."

-N.R.Hart

And, now I don't know
what to do with all
this silence you have
created...
it is a different silence
from the one we once
shared...
I always felt you
near me. Now I am having
some trouble feeling you.
And, I don't know how
to not feel you.

-N.R.Hart

It was a mad passionate
love. A love like that
was unforgettable.
Hearts on fire
always remembering
never forgetting ...
you don't get over a love
like that...
it lives inside you burning
through everything.
Lost lovers hell bent
on finding their way back
again. -N.R.Hart

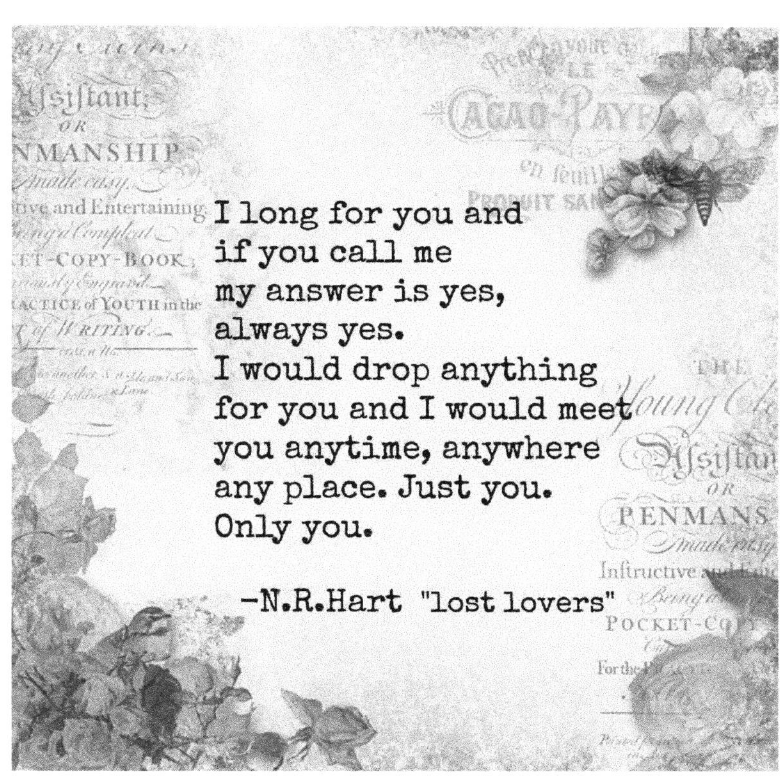
I long for you and
if you call me
my answer is yes,
always yes.
I would drop anything
for you and I would meet
you anytime, anywhere
any place. Just you.
Only you.
-N.R.Hart "lost lovers"

You make me feel things
so many things...
I have never felt before.
You are maddening and
exciting. You thrill me
and you terrify me.
You are impossibly
perfectly you.
But mostly, you are beautiful
and I loved you. I love you
still.
And, I will never love like
this again.
I have never loved like this
before. -N.R.Hart

"love again"

And, if for some reason
I do finally give up on you
just know it took everything
I had and I mean everything
inside me....
how it crushed my heart
killed my soul
I have never fought for anything
the way I fought for you.
I lived and breathed you
and used every last breath
to keep you here with me.
I have died more than once
for you...
and I don't know how many
little deaths I have left in me.
-N.R.Hart "little deaths"

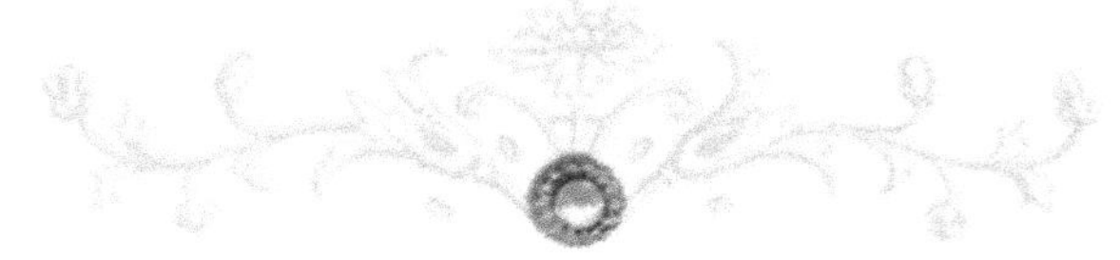

She has this way of
knowing your
feelings
even before they've
had a chance
to surface ... It was
as if she could
feel your soul
long before you do.
-N.R.Hart

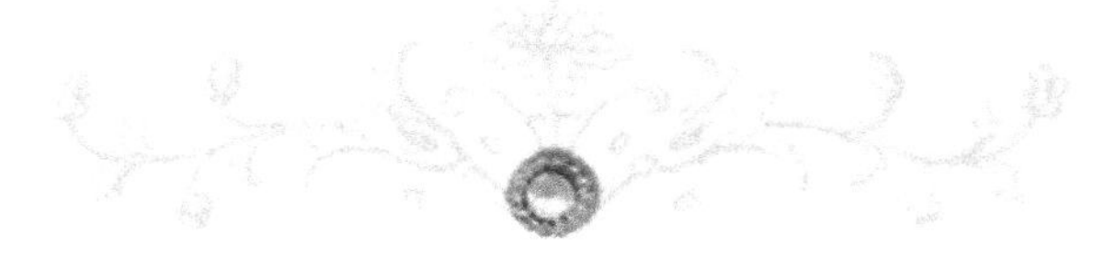

You see I wrote you
these love poems
they were all
stamped with your name
I used poetic verses
but in the end
you never came...
so I could breathe life
Into this poetry
for you to taste my words
one more kiss one last rhyme
one more breath...
for us to love again.
-N.R.Hart

She wanted him in his
rawest form
his rough possession of her
claiming her body
soul on soul sex
branding her with his mouth
his hands
all skin and fire.
This is how the world ends.
This is how love stays alive.

-N.R.Hart

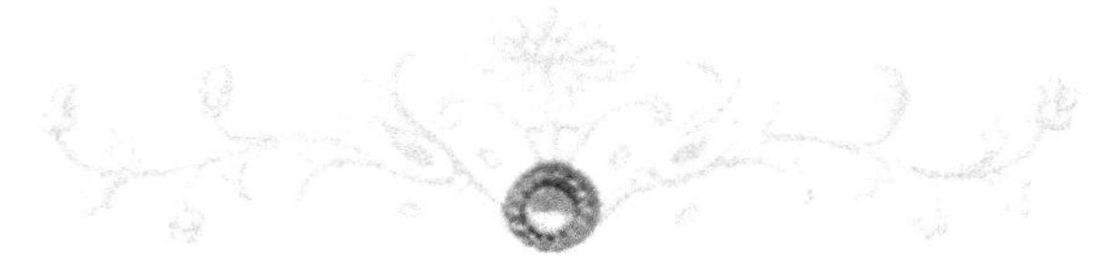

I watched summer
collapse As
it slipped into
fall Desperate
to hold
onto Hot
summer kisses
And Dreamy
moonlight wishes.
-N.R.Hart

I wish I could feel
your hands in my hair
your mouth crushing
down on mine
the weight of your eyes
on me
your soul making love
to mine
Make me feel you. I wish
I could feel you loving me.
I wish...
-N.R.Hart

I don't really wish
to change the world
with the words
I have written
my only wish...
to leave pieces of me
floating about this earth
so those I have touched
have something
to hold onto.
N.R.Hart 01/5/15 "my wish"

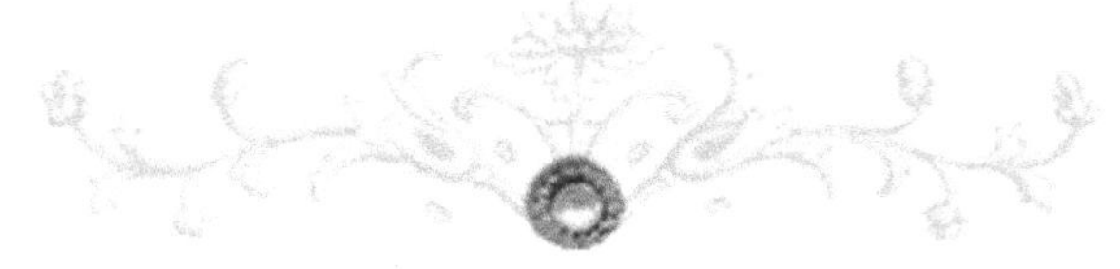

"Goodbye.
Such an impossible word.
One I dare not utter."

N.R.Hart / "unutterable"

Wish upon a star

If I could wish for one
thing, please don't
forget us...
When you look up at the
starry sky remember
those were our stars
lighting up the dark
night the air was our
air smelling of pure
moonlight.
Every time I wish upon
a star you are the only
one there. -N.R.Hart

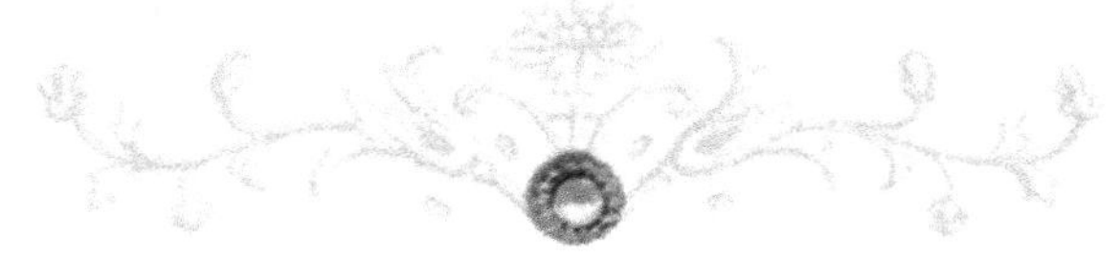

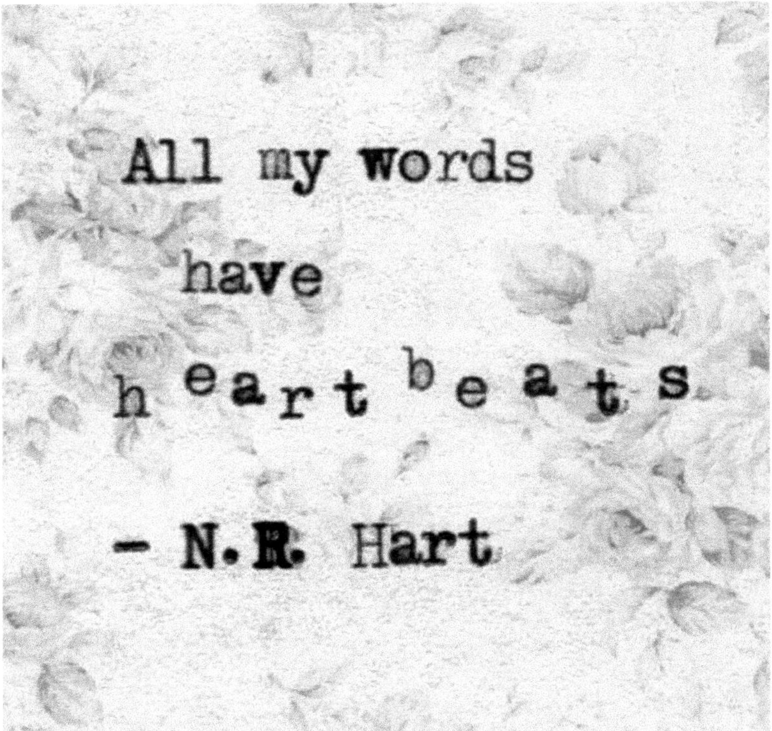

All my words
have
heartbeats
- N.R. Hart

"Seasons of the heart"

And, the seasons change...
a deep winter, a dark blanket
of stars, my melancholy soul
until the warm spring arrives
and with it the fire...
and the beating of my heart
love, romance, violet hyacinths
on my mind...
oh, sweet summertime
I recall the heat in your kiss
and how I was once alive...
and the autumn comes and the leaves
are falling and I am still falling
and these seasons keep changing
but my heart never does. It never
does. And, I still look for you...

-N.R.Hart

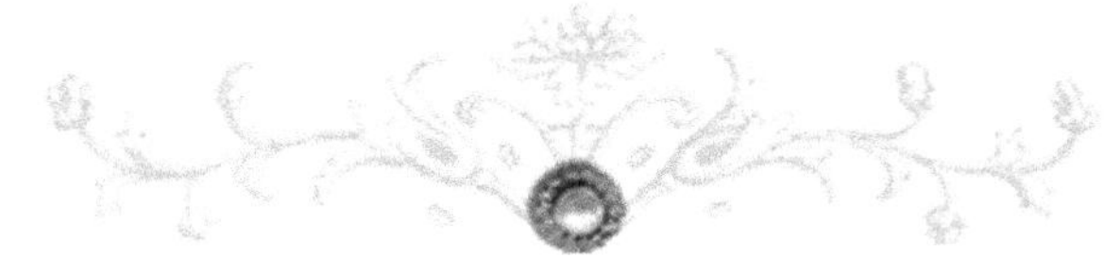

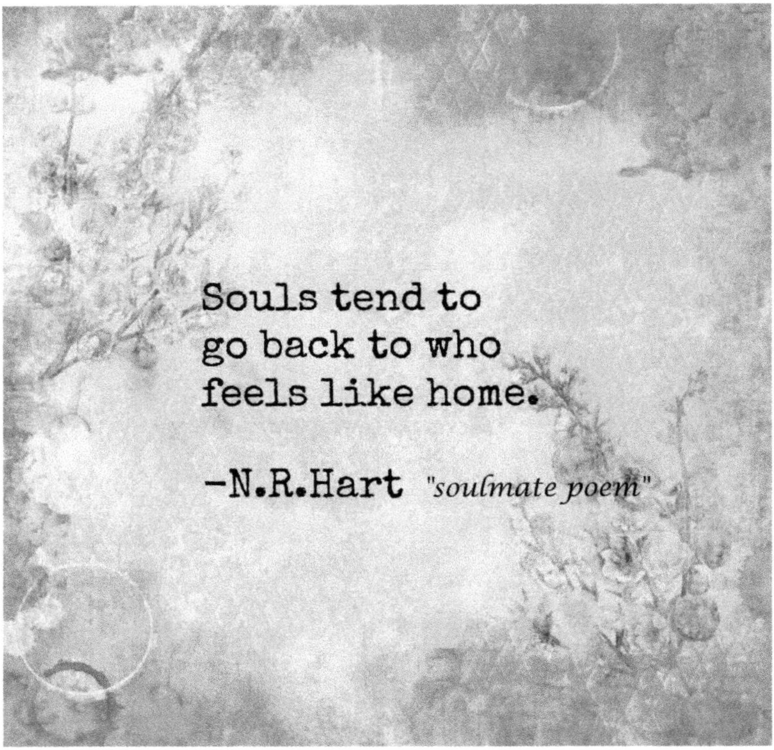

Souls tend to
go back to who
feels like home.

-N.R.Hart *"soulmate poem"*

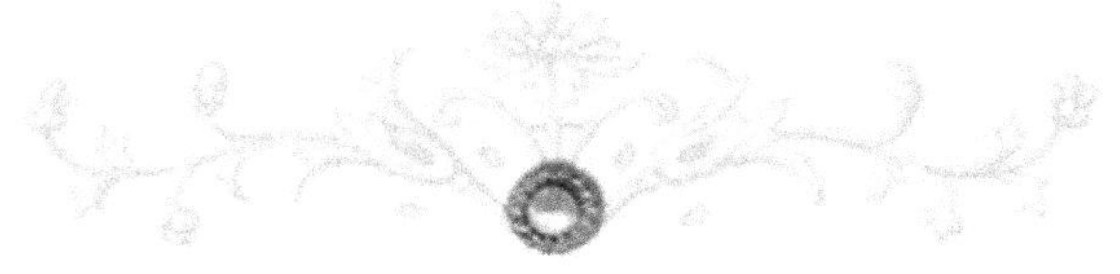

ABOUT THE AUTHOR

N.R.Hart started writing poetry at a young age and used her poetry as a way to express her innermost thoughts and emotions. A true romantic at heart, she expresses feelings of love, hope, passion, despair, vulnerability and romance. Trapping time forever and a keeper of memories is what she loves most about the enduring power of poetry. Her poetry has been so eloquently described as "words delicately placed inside a storm." Poetry is here to make us feel instead of think; as thinking is for the mind and poetry is for the heart and the soul. N.R.Hart hopes to open your heart and touch your soul with her poetry.

"Poets are just romantics who refuse to give up on love." – N.R.Hart

"Only love can save us." – N.R.Hart

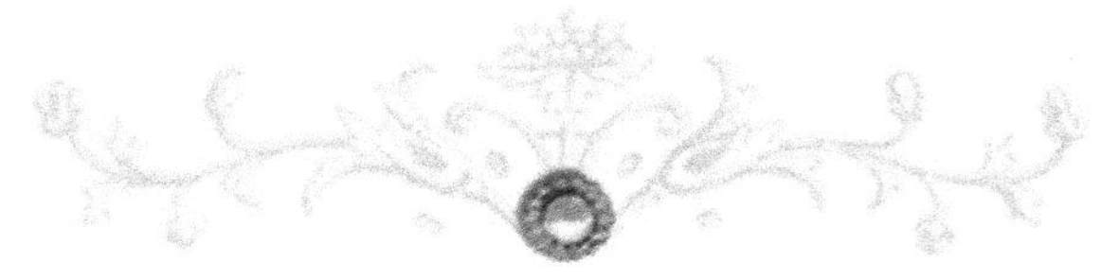

"Poetry is not dead, it is alive
in the minds of those
who feel...instead of think."

N.R.Hart

Connect with N.R.Hart:
FB: N.R.Hart, Author PearlsSlippingOffAString
Instagram: N.R.Hart
Twitter: nrhartpoetry
Tumblr: NRHartAuthor

CPSIA information can be obtained
at www.ICGtesting.com
Printed in the USA
BVHW020608091019
560431BV00024B/697/P